Roscoe Lorenzo Eames

Text-book of light-line shorthand

A practical, phonetic system, without shading

Roscoe Lorenzo Eames

Text-book of light-line shorthand
A practical, phonetic system, without shading

ISBN/EAN: 9783337270681

Printed in Europe, USA, Canada, Australia, Japan

Cover: Foto ©Andreas Hilbeck / pixelio.de

More available books at **www.hansebooks.com**

OF

LIGHT-LINE SHORTHAND.

A PRACTICAL, PHONETIC SYSTEM,

WITHOUT SHADING.

FOR BUSINESS, CORRESPONDENCE, AND VERBATIM REPORTING.

SPECIALLY ADAPTED TO THE USE OF SCHOOLS AND COLLEGES.

BY

ROSCOE L. EAMES,
STENOGRAPHER.

A. S. BARNES & COMPANY,
NEW YORK AND CHICAGO.
1883.

COPYRIGHT, 1883, BY ROSCOE L. EAMES.

M. F. COON, Engraver, 527 Commercial St., San Francisco.

INTRODUCTION.

THE System of Light-line Shorthand is thoroughly and exhaustively presented in this volume. It has now passed through four editions, the first two being in lesson slips, and the third in pamphlet form. After years of study, experiment, and use, during which it has been subjected to the most thorough practical test in the different branches of reporting, Light-line Shorthand, a harmonious and complete whole, is now adequately brought to the notice of learners, and placed within reach of all who may wish to acquire the art of verbatim reporting.

The illustrations are very copious, and both in variety and quantity, are unprecedented in any previous text-book, there being 58 pages of engraved shorthand matter, furnishing an admirable school for practice to the student of Stenography.

The Vocabulary of upwards of 4,500 words and phrases, is ample, and together with the examples embodied in the lessons, gives command of a large proportion of the words used in extemporaneous speaking, besides furnishing abundant analogies for all other words.

The lessons are arranged on the plan of closely combining precept and example. Every principle is practically illustrated, and examples for practice are introduced in the text where they belong, thus demanding attention, and securing the practice which is indispensable to success.

The greatest care has been exercised to present no word to be written until the principles which control the formation of the outline have been explained. Only one style is taught, and that the reporting style, the pupil being conducted by a series of graduated exercises, from the alphabet to the acquirement of all the principles of contraction. The correct and permanent consonant outline is given when a word is first presented, so that the student is freed from the task of afterwards unlearning it, in order to acquire a new and better one. The so-called "Corresponding Style" of shorthand is considered entirely unnecessary for any practical purpose.

The lessons have been prepared with special reference to the necessities of the school and college, and the labor required on the part of the teacher has been reduced to a minimum. This feature enhances, rather than lessens, the desirability of the book as a self-instructor.

A brief statement of the features of the system may be appropriate: It is written without a single *shaded* character; it assigns horizontal and slanting upward curves to the representation of the most frequently recurring sounds; the cognate sounds are represented by lines struck in the same direction, but *short* and *long* for the *whispered* and *voiced* sounds respectively; the signs are never halved nor lengthened, and only three sizes of stems are used, namely, tick, short, and long; the system is unapproachable in ease of execution, and its exceeding legibility is largely consequent from this flexibility, for an outline that is easily executed is not liable to be distorted when written at a high rate of speed ; six stems may be struck in two directions, thus securing the greatest possible lineality, and, together with the frequency of curved lines, insuring acute angles in almost all cases where angles are necessary. The system conforms to the great law of *Curve Motion,* which is also the law of muscular motion.

The Connecting Hook of this system cuts the Gordian Knot of bad joinings, and renders otherwise awkward and difficult forms as rapid and legible as any.

The absence of shading, *per se*, adds at least twenty-five per cent. to speed, and fifty per cent. to legibility.

The true status of Phrase-writing is herein fixed, and that much-vaunted practice relieved from the empiricism and obscurity in which it has been shrouded. Instead of the wholesale advice too often proffered by shorthand authors, to phrase under all conceivable circumstances, its real value and mode of application is plainly stated.

A valuable arrangement of Connective Vowels is presented—the result of two years labor in this particular direction, after a practical knowledge of all modern schemes of a like nature. They combine the advantages of joining, and "pointing in," and may be generally connected where most needed, at the beginning or end of words of but one consonant sound. The vowel sounds of the language are subjected to a rigorous practical analysis, and the assignment of material to their representation, and their grouping in three positions, will be found of the utmost value to the verbatim reporter.

The system presents an entirely new arrangement of Stenographic Principles of Contraction, making improved use of the old, and introducing new and valuable material. It is chiefly in consequence of this that the objectionable features of *shading* and *halving* have been successfully eliminated. In this connection reference is made more especially to the Medium-sized circle, the Inclosed circle, the Divided circle, the Large loop, the Extension curl, the Lengthening principle, and the Compound curve.

As a single illustration of the improved use of material, it may be stated that the medium-sized circle (equally as valuable as the small circle) is assigned in Phonography to the sound of ss or sz, occurring only five times in 1,400 words, while in the New System that circle is assigned to the sound of N, occurring about 500 times in 1,400 words. This material is as good as thrown away in Phonography.

Aside from the advantage of light lines, the new system is manifestly superior in its lineality, and in its desirable frequency of acute angles. Among other points of superiority, Light-line Shorthand provides the best forms for the most common words, and gives the shorter form for the shorter combination of sounds, and *vice versa*.

From long experience, the Author's facilities for teaching by mail make this method fully equal to personal instruction. Although the book is a thorough self-instructor, yet a course of lessons by a competent teacher will many times repay their cost in the abridgment of the time necessary for the acquirement of the system.

Teachers should use their own judgment in the assignment of lessons, though in the first part of the book they are believed to be fairly proportioned. Subsequent lessons are made longer or shorter, in order to exhaust the particular subject only of which they treat.

Good materials for practice are ruled paper, with lines at least one-third of an inch apart, with but little gloss on the surface, and a pencil of medium quality. Pen and ink may be used if desirable, but their employment is exceptional among reporters.

I acknowledge my indebtedness in the elaboration of this system to the various Phonographic and other writers on Shorthand, and especially to John Brown Smith, that bold pioneer in the new era of Stenography, whose original and acute mind first perceived and applied the scientific principles of Curve Motion in shorthand writing.

ROSCOE L. EAMES.

SAN FRANCISCO, *January, 1883.*

LIGHT-LINE SHORTHAND.

LESSON I.

1. The sounds of the English language are divided into two principal classes, obstructed sounds and free sounds. The former are called Consonants, and the latter Vowels. To illustrate: in the following words the consonants are represented by italics and the vowels by Roman letters: p*ill*, *b*a*g*, *r*o*b*.

2. In this system of shorthand there are no silent letters, but each letter has an invariable power. In order to represent a word in shorthand, it must first be resolved into its elements, or phonetically analyzed; then the signs representing the actual sounds heard must be written. For instance, in the word *rogue*, phonetic analysis discloses but three sounds, *rog*, the *ue* being silent; in *laugh*, only *laf* are found, and the words should be written accordingly.

NOTE 1.—It will be seen that the common orthography is misleading, and that the first task of the student will be to free himself from the slavery of the common spelling, and to learn to analyze words into their actual elementary sounds.

3. As in this system words are chiefly represented by the consonant outline, or skeleton, the vowels being generally omitted, the consonants, occupying as they do, the place of chief importance, are presented first.

4. The consonants of the English language are divided, according to their character, into six classes, called Abrupts,

Continuants, Liquids, Nasals, Coalescents, and the Aspirate.

5. The Abrupts are those in which the breath is completely obstructed in passing the organs of speech. They are eight in number, and are represented as follows:

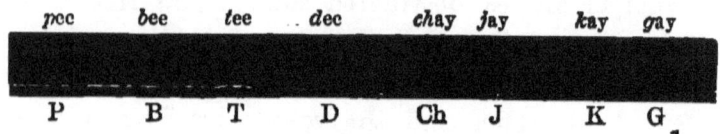

Their names are given immediately above the Plate, the italic letters in the names showing their sounds, or powers. For convenience and economy of illustration, each shorthand sign is represented by a letter of the common alphabet. These type letters are called "Stenotypes." They are shown immediately below the Plate. All alphabetical shorthand consonant forms are called stems or strokes.

DIRECTION OF WRITING.—LENGTH.

6. P and B should be struck upward, T and D from left to right, and Ch, J, K, and G downward. The short stems should be one-eighth, and the long stems one-quarter of an inch in length. Each of these stems should be a quarter of a circle.

Note 2.—For blackboard writing, of course, a larger scale must be fixed upon, but the relative proportions of the signs should be maintained.

Note 3.—P and B, when joined to other stems, may sometimes be written downward, as explained further on. When standing alone, they should always be written as directed in Par. 6.

Note 4.—Observe that similar sounds are represented by similar lines. The Cognate sounds (those produced by the same organic movement, but differing only in being whispered or voiced) being represented by lines struck in the same direction, but *short* and *long* for the *whispered* and *voiced* sounds respectively. Thus, P and B are pronounced by the same organic movement, but P is whispered, while B is voiced; so with T and D, Ch and J, K and G. These observations refer, of course, to the actual powers of these letters, as heard in a given word, not to their alphabetical names. The sound of P, for instance, may be discovered by pronouncing the word "cap," then dropping the *c*, we have "ap," then the *a*, and we have the true sound of P. A similar process with the word "cab" will disclose the true sound of B.

NOTE 5.—Drill on these characters until their forms and names are readily associated. Let the teacher write a stem on the blackboard, the class giving its name. This exercise may be varied by the teacher pronouncing a letter while one of the class gives a description, as: Teacher, "P"; Pupil, "Northwest, curve, short," (describing the part of the circle which the letter forms). Teacher, "D"; Pupil, "North, curve, long," etc. Pupils should be drilled in writing, either on the blackboard, or with pencil or pen and paper, in the latter case passing their exercises to the teacher for correction at his leisure, or the teacher may make the corrections by writing the proper forms on the board, the class observing and making their own corrections.

LESSON II.

7. The Continuants, or second class of consonants, involve less obstruction to the breath, or voice, in pronunciation, than the Abrupts. They are represented as follows:

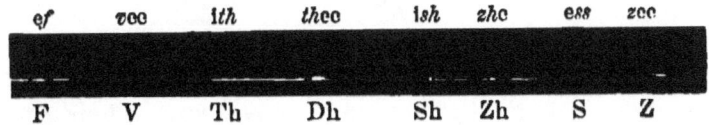

As in Par. 5, the names and powers of the signs are given above the Plate, and the Stenotypes below.

NOTE 6.—It will be seen that F and V are cognates, as also Th and Dh, Sh and Zh, and S and Z.

DIRECTION OF WRITING.—LENGTH.

8. F and V should be struck upward. Th and Dh from left to right, and Sh, Zh, S, and Z downward. Their lengths are the same as those of the short and long stems representing the Abrupts, as explained in Par. 6. Each of these stems should be a quarter of a circle.

NOTE 7.—F and V, when joined to other stems, may sometimes be struck downward, as subsequently explained. When standing alone, they should always be written as directed in Par. 8. The remarks on the Abrupts in Note 4 apply also to these consonant forms.

NOTE 8.—Drill on these signs as directed in Note 5 until they become familiar. It will be well, also, to introduce as part of this lesson a review drill on the forms given in Lesson I.

LESSON III.

REMAINING CONSONANTS.

9. The four remaining classes of consonants, comprising the Liquids R and L, the Nasals M, N, and Ng, the Coalescents W and Y, and the Aspirate H, are represented as follows:

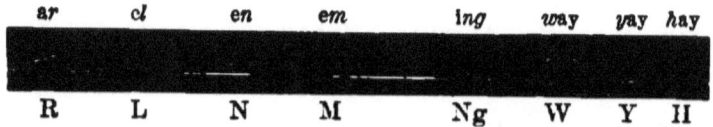

Their names are given above the Plate, the italic letters in the names showing their sounds or powers. Their Stenotypes are shown immediately below the Plate. The hook of L may be written on either side of the stem, according to convenience, and should always be at the beginning of the stem. The most convenient side for the hook will be on the left when the stem is not connected with any other form. The wave signs Ng, W, and Y have two forms, as shown above, and may be reversed so as to curve the other way, when necessary to make an easy joining with other forms.

DIRECTION OF STRIKING.—LENGTH.

10. R and L should be struck upward, N and W from left to right, and M, Ng, Y, and H downward. Each stem

in this Plate should be one-eighth of an inch in length, or the same as the short stems shown in Pars. 5 and 7.

NOTE 9.—R and L may sometimes be written downward as subsequently explained.

NOTE 10.—Drill on these signs until they become familiar. R and L may be described as "Northeast," and "Northeast hooked," N "East," M "Southeast," and Ng, W and Y as "Southeast," "East," and "South" waves respectively; H "South." A review of Lessons I and II can be advantageously introduced here.

NOTE 11.—The Liquids are so called from their peculiar sound resembling the flowing of a liquid. The Nasals are so named because the breath passes through the nasal passages in their pronunciation. The Coalescents are so called from their facility of uniting with other sounds. The Aspirate, as its name implies, is a rough breathing.

11. As an aid to recalling the consonant signs, the following diagram will be of use:

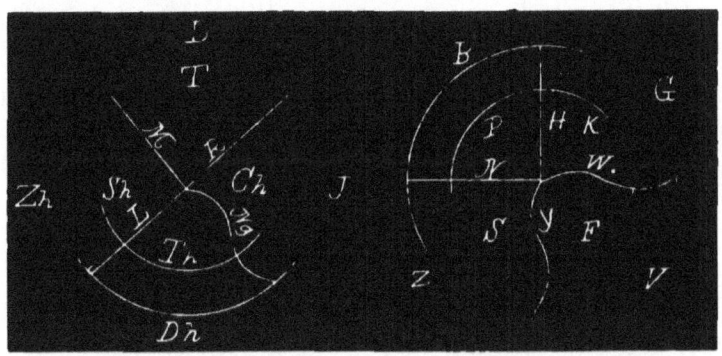

T may be remembered by observing that it forms the T-op of the circle; then D, its cognate, will be readily suggested. Th and its cognate Dh may be remembered as occupying the exact opposite quarter, or the sou-TH of the circle. P may be remembered as the prominent sound in u-P, it being the "up" curve. The different radii of the circle give the forms assigned to the Liquids, Nasals, Coalescents, and Aspirate.

By familiarizing these maps of the consonant alphabet, the learner will be greatly assisted at first in recalling the alphabetic forms.

LESSON IV.

VOWELS.

12. The three pairs of vowels pronounced through a *widened* mouth aperture are represented as follows:

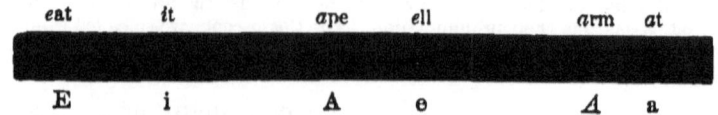

The names and sounds of these signs are the same, and are heard in the words given above the Plate, the italic letters representing their sounds and names. Their Stenotypes are given below the Plate, and consist of capital and small Roman letters, with the exception of the vowel *A* which is represented by an italic capital.

DIRECTION OF STRIKING.—LENGTH.

13. E and i should be struck upward, A from left to right, and *A* and a downward. e is a small dot. When joined to other forms E and i may be written up or down, whichever direction affords the best angle of joining. The dash signs should be one-sixteenth of an inch in length, and the dot for e as small as can be made conveniently. Each of the curved signs should be a quarter of a circle. When E and i are struck downward their Stenotypes are printed in italics.

Note 12.—The length of these vowel signs as compared with the consonant forms is as follows: The vowels E, i, A, *A*, and a should be one-half the length of the short consonant stems. So in blackboard writing their lengths must be proportioned to the scale of length adopted for the consonant stems.

Note 13.—These vowel signs are paired, as were the consonants, although they are not perfect cognates. The remarks in Note 4 apply generally to these signs, though the difference between the cognate sounds is in length rather than quality.

NOTE 14.—A drill may be had on these vowel signs similar to that on the consonants. Use the word "tick" for the straight vowel A, and "tick curve" for the others except e, which may be called the "dot." Let the teacher pronounce E; the pupil describes it as "Southeast tick curve"; teacher, A; pupil, "tick East," etc.

14. Consonants and vowels are joined together in writing in their natural order, except when an awkward angle would result at the point of joining, when it is better to disjoin the vowel and write it beside the consonant stem, as explained hereafter. Write all words whose prominent vowel is E or i above the line, as follows:

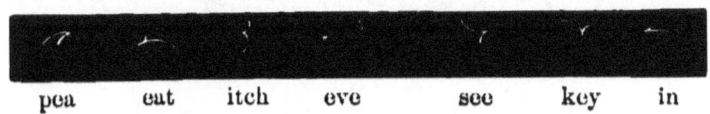

pea   eat   itch   eve   see   key   in

A distinct joining must be made between consonants and vowels—that is, they must join at an angle, and the best angle is the sharpest, because most easily formed, as any one can readily discover by experiment. Write the following exercise rapidly, and the superiority of acute angles over obtuse will be at once manifest:

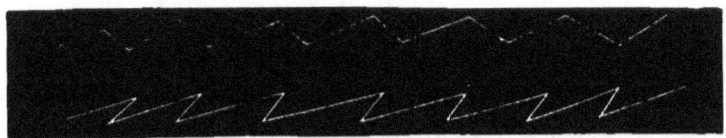

In order to insure the best angle of joining in all cases, the vowels E and i may be used interchangeably, either at the beginning or end of words. No difficulty in reading connected writing will be experienced from this practice, as these cognate sounds are not liable to conflict.

NOTE 15.—The reason for the three positions assigned to words in this lesson will be explained at the proper time.

EXAMPLES.—Bee, tea, each, eke, if, fee, thee, she, ease, easy, e'en, knee, me, wee, ye, he.

NOTE 16.—The practice of writing from dictation should be adopted at once and steadily adhered to. No exercise should be passed over until it has become fairly familiar. At the outset, let the rule be established to read everything that is written repeatedly. Let the drill in reading be always as thorough as that in writing. This advice cannot be too highly commended, for nowhere does practical success depend more on "making haste slowly" than in this matter of reading whatever is written.

15. Write all words whose prominent vowel is A or e on the line, as follows:

Abe   eddy   etch   gay   fay   say   nay   hay

When a vowel does not make a distinct joining with a consonant stem, it must be disjoined and written beside the stem, according to the following rule:

16. For a vowel to read *before* a stem, it must be written to the *left* of a *vertical* or *inclined* stem, and *above* a *horizontal;* for a vowel to read *after* a stem, it must be written to the *right* of a *vertical* or *inclined* stem, and *below* a *horizontal*. The vowel should be written near the stem but not touching it, and to avoid, as far as possible, a retrograde motion of the pencil; it should be written near the end of the stem where the pencil stops. This is called "pointing in" the vowels. Of course the dot e will always be pointed in. The Stenotype of this pointing in is a colon.

EXAMPLES.—Ape, pay, bay, ebb, day, edge, age, jay, ache, egg, they, may, aim, way, away, yea.

NOTE 17.—The position of a word, whether above, on the line, or otherwise, is determined by the position of the consonant stem, and not by that of the vowel. The vowel accommodates itself to the position of the consonant.

17. Write all words whose prominent vowel is *A* or a through the line if the consonant stem is vertical or in-

clinĕd, and on the line if the stem is horizontal, as follows:

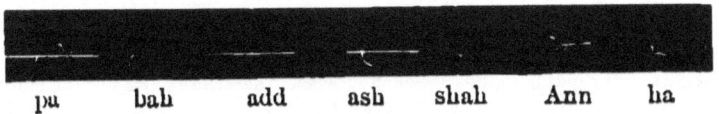

| pa | bah | add | ash | shah | Ann | ha |

A and *a* may be written interchangeably to secure good angles, in the same manner as E and i, as heretofore explained.

EXAMPLES.—Abbey, Addie, Aggie, ashy, Anna, Annie, am, ma.

LESSON V.
VOWELS.

18. The three pairs of vowels pronounced through a *rounded* mouth aperture are represented as follows:

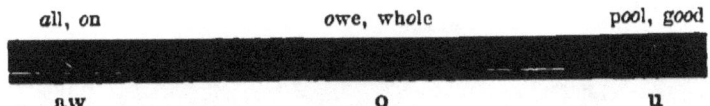

| all, on | owe, whole | pool, good |
| aw | o | u |

The names and sounds of these signs are the same, and are heard in the words given above the Plate, the italic letters representing their sounds and names. Their Stenotypes are given below the Plate, and consist of small, or lower-case Roman letters.

NOTE 18.—Only one sign is given to represent the long and short sounds of the vowel in each case, the cognates being perfect and differing only in length. This scheme is entirely practicable.

DIRECTION OF STRIKING.—LENGTH.

19. aw and o should be struck downward, and u from left to right. The dashes aw and o should be one-sixteenth

of an inch in length, and the half-circle u one thirty-second of an inch across, and should form a half-circle as its description indicates.

NOTE 19.—Drill on these signs until they become familiar. Let the teacher pronounce aw; the pupil replies "tick Southeast," describing the direction toward which the sign is struck; the teacher pronounces u; the pupil answers "small half-circle North," describing the portion of a circle which it forms.

20. Write all words whose prominent vowel is aw above the line, as follows:

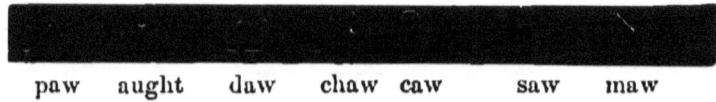

paw   aught   daw   chaw   caw   saw   maw

Disjoin the vowel when it will not make a distinct angle, and point it in as shown in Par. 16.

EXAMPLES—Jaw, off, thaw, Shaw, raw, gnaw, Waugh, yaw, haw.

21. Write all words whose prominent vowel is o on the line, as follows:

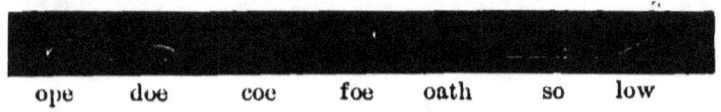

ope   doe   coe   foe   oath   so   low

Point in the vowel when it does not join well.

EXAMPLES.—Poe, bow, toe, Joe, oak, oaf, though, show, row, own, mow, woe, hoe.

22. Write all words whose prominent vowel is u through the line if the consonant stem is vertical or inclined, and on the line if the stem is horizontal, as follows:

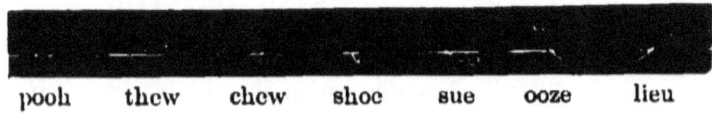

pooh   thew   chew   shoe   sue   ooze   lieu

This vowel may open up or down; use that form which gives the most acute angle in joining with other forms—either the North, or the South half-circle.

EXAMPLES.—Adieu, Jew, rue, anew.

LESSON VI.

VOWELS.

23. The obscure vowel in her, the natural vowel in up, and the double vowels in by, boy, bough, and few, called diphthongs, are represented as follows:

her, up	tie	toy	cow	view
eu	I	awi	ow	iu

The names and sounds of these signs are the same, and are heard in the words given above the Plate, the italic letters representing their sounds and names. Their Stenotypes are given below the Plate.

DIRECTION OF STRIKING.—LENGTH.

24. When standing alone, eu and I should be struck upward, awi from left to right, ow downward, and iu downward and left to right. When joined to other stems, eu and I may be written up or down according to convenience of joining. When written contrary to the direction given here, their Stenotypes are printed in italics.

The signs eu, I, and ow should be one-sixteenth of an inch in length. The compound signs awi and iu, formed of the simple signs aw and i, and i and u respectively, have their component parts the same length as the simple signs which form them. eu and ow have reverse forms for convenience in joining, either of which may be used.

Note 20.—It is not necessary, except where great accuracy is required, to write the diphthong iu, the sign u being generally all that is needed.

Note 21.—In drilling on these signs, eu and ow may be described as "tick waves," I as "tick Northeast," and awi and iu by adopting the description of their component parts if desirable.

25. Write all words whose prominent vowel is eu or awi on the line, as follows:

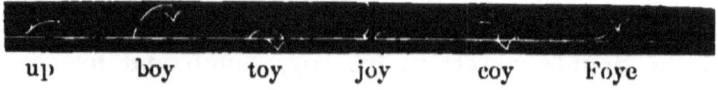

up   boy   toy   joy   coy   Foye

eu will always make a good joining by reversing it when necessary. Point in awi when it does not join well.

EXAMPLES.—Roy, annoy, ahoy.

26. Write all words whose prominent vowel is I above the line, as follows:

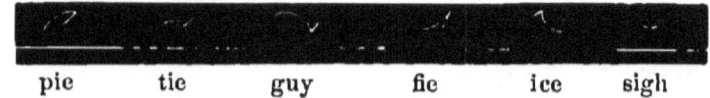

pie   tie   guy   fie   ice   sigh

A good angle may always be secured by joining the upward or downward form of this vowel.

EXAMPLES.—Buy, die, vie, ivy, thigh, thy, shy, icy, nigh, my, rye, lie, high.

27. Write all words whose prominent vowel is ow or iu through the line if the consonant stem is vertical or inclined, and on the line if the stem is horizontal, as follows:

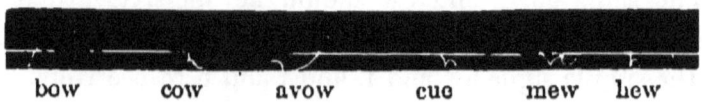

bow   cow   avow   cue   mew   hew

ow may always be joined by a choice of its forms. The same is true of iu, which may be reduced, generally, to its last element u. In the word "mew" it is necessary to write iu in full, to distinguish the word from "moo," with which it might conflict. iu may be reversed as shown in the Plate.

EXAMPLES.—Dow, ouch, vow, sow, row, mow, how, pew, few, view.

28. Two vowels occurring together are represented by their signs joined, and written in their natural order, as follows:

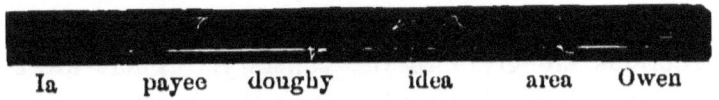

| Ia | payee | doughy | idea | area | Owen |

For this purpose e may be represented by its mate A to admit of joining, as in the word "Owen."

In case of two or more vowels in a word, the position of the word is determined by the prominent or accented vowel. A word consisting altogether of vowels should be written on the line. Disjoin the vowels as usual when a good angle cannot be secured.

EXAMPLES.—Io, boa, Bowie, iota, dewey, Coey, Iago, via, thawy, Zoe, showy, Owen, Hoey.

LESSON VII.

RECAPITULATION.—GENERAL VIEW.

29. All the alphabetical principles have now been explained, and it will be in order to present a general view of the alphabet, for purposes of reference and thorough comprehension. In the Plate on page 189 the alphabet is shown as a whole, the first column showing the shorthand conso-

nant signs, the second their names, the third their Stenotypes, the fourth a common word containing the sound of each letter, the fifth the direction in which each stem should be written, and the sixth the vowels with their Stenotypes.

30. It has been seen that all words are written in one of three positions—above, on, or through the line, according to the prominent vowel. These three positions are named First, Second, and Third; the First position being *above*, the Second *on*, and the Third *through* the line of writing. This rule of writing words in position must be strictly adhered to throughout this book, except where special instructions are given to the contrary. There are some words consisting of horizontal stems that are written immediately under the line, which is the real Third position for horizontals, but they are exceptions to the general rule, and will be noted in the lists of word signs and in the Vocabulary. It is generally unnecessary to write words beginning with horizontal stems in the Third position.

31. The object of writing words in position in this way is to enable the advanced writer to generally omit the vowels, and still retain legibility. All words are thus assigned to three general classes, two or three principal vowels being prominent in each class. The diphthongs are usually written.

32. The following table will exhibit the vowels assigned to each position:

Nothing will obviate the necessity of acquiring thorough familiarity with this classification of the vowels and the positions of words determined by them. Writing in position must be carefully observed until the practice becomes automatic.

NOTE 22.—Let the teacher use his judgment as to the necessity of introducing a thorough review of the preceding instruction at this point, giving drills on all the alphabetical elements. It will be a loss of time to take up new features until those already presented have become the property of the learner. Above all, let the learner not omit to read everything he writes again and again. Reading and writing must keep equal pace.

LESSON VIII.

JOINING OF STEMS.

33. For greater economy and convenience, the Plates illustrating the following lessons will be given in the latter part of the book. The lines of shorthand characters will be numbered and referred to accordingly. This lesson is illustrated by the Plate on page 190.

34. All the consonants in a word consisting of two or more stems are usually written without lifting the pen, the second beginning where the first ends, and so on until all are written.

LINE 1.—PP, PK, PCh, P*L*, TD, TCh, ThSh, RL, LR, MM.

35. Printing Stenotypes continuously without anything between them indicates that the signs they represent are joined. Printing with a hyphen between indicates that they are to be disjoined and written near together, whether consonants or vowels. When a vowel is to be pointed in, its Stenotype is separated from that of the consonant by a colon.

NOTE 23.—Stenotypes in parenthesis will be occasionally introduced in the following exercises in this book to show the way in which a word should be written; sometimes the form of the whole word will be so indicated, and sometimes only one consonant or vowel requiring special attention. Vowels so indicated should never be omitted.

EXAMPLES.—BB, BJ, PSh, BG, BZ, TB, DT, DK, DSh, DZ, ChP, JT, ChCh, JK, ChM, JN, JNg, KP, GT, KJ, KK, KW, GSh, GZ, ThSh, ThM, ThNg, ST, SNg, ShD, RR, LL, NZh, NZ, NN, NM, NNg, NH, NgK, YT, YK, YM, HT, HJ, HK, HSh, HN, HM, HNg, HH.

NOTE 24.—No confusion will result from printing the Stenotypes consecutively, since the small "h" and "g" are never used except in the Stenotypes Th, Sh, Ng, etc.

NOTE 25.—In joining the waves W, Y, and Ng to other consonants, use that form which makes the best joining with a preceding or following stem.

36. When vowels occur between consonants that are joined, it is usually better to point in such vowels. This method obviates the necessity of breaking the consonant outline, and adds to speed. In pointing in the vowels, as here directed, it should be done with as little retrograde motion as possible; and although a vowel will read properly whether written after the first or before the second consonant, it will generally be more convenient to write it before the second, to avoid carrying the hand back.

37. The *first* stem, in a word consisting of more than one stem, is written in position according to the accented vowel of the word, the other stems following and accommodating themselves to the position of this first stem. Third position words of more than one stem, the first being horizontal, have that first stem written on the line.

LINE 2.—Tack, check, cog, chyme, noon, mock, mug, yacht, hook, hot.

NOTE 26.—The words in Line 2 are written in position, as will be seen, according to the accented vowel. The rule of position must always be observed in the examples following in this book.

EXAMPLES.—Chalk, choke, chuck, cheek, chick, chum, Jack, joke, jog, jig, jam, caulk, cake, coke, cook, keg, catch, coach, ketch, cage, kedge, calm, comb, gawk, gag, gig, gouge, gage, gang, gong, game, Mack, Mike, muck, Mag, maim, yoke, yam, hack, hawk, hag, hog, hatch, hitch, hedge, hang, hung, ham, hum, home, hymn, talk, duke, dog, thumb, tuck, tick, tag, tug, tap, top, type, tape, tip, tongue, dock, dike, deck, duck, dug, dig, deep, dip, dupe, dab, daub, dub, dodge, adage, Doge, thatch, thong, theme, gnash, numb, nun, nine.

LESSON IX.

JOINING OF STEMS.

(Illustrated by the Plate on page 190.)

38. There are a few cases where stems, if joined in the ordinary way, would show no angle, or a very slight angle at the point of connection, and in which the individuality of the stems would be somewhat obscured. In order to insure legibility and speed, special treatment of these cases is necessary. They are governed by the following rule:

39. When necessary to preserve the distinctive shape of connected stems, the joining should be made by a hook attached to one of the stems and written as follows: Between a curve and a straight stem, the hook should be attached to the curve; between two curves, the hook should be attached to the first curve. The Stenotype of this connecting hook is a small or lower-case c.

LINE 3.—Tomb, Adam, match, Josie, teething, thick.

NOTE 27.—Vowels at the beginning or end of words should be joined when convenient.

EXAMPLES.—Tom, tame, team, dime, dame, dummy, dome, dim, deem, towage, toothache, Dutch, ditch, Edith, Idaho, Jewish, cozy, ethic, image, Madge, midget, myth, mouth, shame, sham, shiny, huzza.

40. In many cases the form of the word will indicate the distinctive shape of the stems, and render the use of the connecting hook unnecessary.

LINE 4.—Back, pack, being, teeth, defy, death.

NOTE 28.—In the case of an outline like the word "back," as shown in Line 4, the form of the word shows that the first stem is B, and the second K, since if both were long or both short, the bottoms of the two stems would be even horizontally, as in the next word "pack," in Line 4, in which both stems are short. The different stems are plainly shown in the remaining words of the line. The stems in the word "death" are made sufficiently plain by increasing the curvature of the stem Th.

EXAMPLES.—Patch, pouch, poach, podge, page, apogee, peck, pock, opaque, poke, peg, epic (e), peevish, pang, aping, pung, batch, botch, balk, bake, aback, beck, book, big, bog, bug, buggy, bag, boggy, beg, bang, bung, teach, touch, tooth, shake, shook, ask.

LESSON X.

JOINING OF STEMS.—STEMS STRUCK IN TWO DIRECTIONS.

(Illustrated by the Plate on page 190.)

41. The six stems, P, B, F, V, R, and L, may sometimes be struck downward, as heretofore stated. The Stenotypes of the downward forms are printed in italics. The ordinary slant of these six stems when struck upward is about thirty degrees with the line of writing, but when struck downward their slant is considerably less, being about sixty degrees with the line.

NOTE 29.—This difference in slant, although not very apparent in respect of the curves, and not essential in their case, is plainly seen in the case of the straight stems. This varying slant results from the natural laws of motion, which, in writing, subordinate all upward, downward, and backward movements to the onward direction of the writing.

42. The six stems above mentioned may be struck downward when necessary to secure a better joining with a preceding or following stem.

Line 5.—Pithy, bathe, fiat, veto, riot, Elliott.

Line 6.—Reap, Zebedee, puffy, review, theory, delay.

Note 30.—Of course, where there is a choice of joinings, the best will at once be obvious, acute angles being much superior to obtuse. The best joining is *no* angle; the next best an acute angle.

Examples.—Path, apathy, pith, both, bath, Booth, ebony, folk, fag, fog, foggy, fig, fetch, Fitch, fudge, fidget, effigy, food, funny, vouch, evoke, vague, vogue, road, ruddy, rack, rock, rake, wreak, reck, wreck, rick, rig, rag, renew, Reno, asp, ship, shape, shop, nip, neap, nap, shabby, nib, nob, bevy, envy, navy, thorough, authority, theorem, sherry, Ezra, zero, narrow, inroad, enrich, energy, enormity, pillow, Polly, Apollo, Paley, pulley, Polk, polka, billow, bellow, below, belly, belay, Bailey, by-law, bully, Billy, belie, bilk, bulk, bulky, tally, tallow, outlaw, outlay, outlie, Italy, Italian, dally, dolly, daily, duly, Chili, chilly, jolly, jelly, callow, Kelly, gaily, galley, gully, ugly, yellow, hilly, highly, hallow, hollow, holly, halo, alike, elk, Illinois, Caleb, colic, colleague, Galena, italic, dilemma, deluge, pillage, apology, Pollock, belch, bilge, bulge, Amalek, Malacca, Malaga.

Note 31.—Every word should be fully vocalized, since this practice is absolutely necessary to insure thorough familiarity with the vowels and the method of pointing them in. The learner will be advised when the proper time comes to begin omitting the vowels.

43. It is a great aid to legibility when vowels are omitted, if the place where the vowel occurs can be indicated. This can be done in the case of the stems R and L, when standing alone, in the following way:

44. When R or L is the only consonant in a word, and is preceded by a vowel, the stem should be struck downward at an angle of about sixty degrees with the line of writing.

Line 7.—Are, ear, arrow, ell, eel, ill, allay.

Examples.—Air, era, Erie, airy, array, or, Ira, awry, err, ally, Eli, alloy, allow.

45. When joined to a following stem and preceded by a vowel, and the upward or downward forms of these two

stems will join equally well, they should be written downward, as shown in Par. 44.

LINE 8.—Army, herb, urge, alum, Elba, Alpha.

EXAMPLES.—Aroma, orb, Oreb, Arab, Arabia, airily, airing, elm, Alamo, Alma, Elijah, allege, elegy, Alp, clope, alibi, elbow, Alva, Oolong.

46. When R or L is the only consonant in a word, and is not preceded by a vowel, the stem should be struck upward at an angle of about thirty degrees with the line of writing.

LINE 9.—Ray, raw, row, lay, lee, low.

EXAMPLES.—Rue, rye, Roy, row, lie, lieu, lea.

47. When joined to a following stem, and not preceded by a vowel, and the upward or downward form of the letter R will join equally well, it should be written upward, as shown in Par. 46.

NOTE 32.—L is not used in this situation except in certain special cases, which will be given in the proper place. The method of writing initial L in words of more than one consonant will be shown further on.

LINE 10.—Reap, reach, review, Rory, rely, room, ring.

EXAMPLES.—Rip, ripe, rap, rob, rib, rope, robe, rub, ruby, rupee, rich, wretch, ridge, rage, ream, rim, rhyme, Rome, roam, rum, ram, rheum, roomy, wrung, rang, wrong.

48. When R occurs at the end of a word, being joined to a preceding stem, and both upward and downward forms are equally convenient, the stem should be struck upward if a vowel follows, and downward if no vowel follows it.

The occurrence of the stem L in this situation almost invariably indicates that it is followed by a vowel; therefore it may be struck up or down. The exceptions to this rule will be noted hereafter.

NOTE 33.—The method of indicating final L with no vowel following will be subsequently explained

LINE 11.—Fair, ferry, Avery, Rarey, roar, merry, gaily, folly.

NOTE 34.—The proper direction and a good joining may sometimes be secured by reversing a preceding stem when allowable, as in the case of the words "fair" and "ferry," in Line 11.

EXAMPLES.—Fare, fear, fairy, fury, farrow, furrow, marrow, marry, miry, morrow, Mary, Murray, emery, rear, rare, Aurora, volley, villa, mellow, Molly, Milo, Emily, rally, Rolla, Raleigh, Riley.

LESSON XI.

BRIEF SIGNS FOR S, Z, N.—FORWARD AND BACKWARD MOTION.

49. FORWARD AND BACKWARD MOTION.—To facilitate illustration throughout the remaining lessons, the terms Forward and Backward Motion will be employed. Forward Motion is with, and Backward Motion contrary to, the motion of the hands of a clock, as shown in the following diagrams:

BACKWARD MOTION.

FORWARD MOTION.

The arrow-points show the direction in which the forms are struck.

50. Although the alphabetic forms which have now been fully explained would enable the learner to write any word in the language, the long forms which would be required

for many words would render verbatim reporting impossible. Therefore, in addition to the stem forms which have been assigned, speed requires shorter signs for certain frequently recurring consonant sounds. These requirements are met in the case of the sounds of S, Z, and N, as follows:

51. The sound of S or Z is indicated by a very small circle attached to stems at either end, and read in the order in which it is written. It is turned on the inside of curves, as follows:

sPs　sDs　sChs　sKs　sVs　sThs　sShs　sZs

The Stenotype of this circle, whether used for S or Z, is a small or lower-case s.

NOTE 35.—No difficulty is experienced in using this sign for both S and Z, except in certain cases where Z occurs initially, hereafter provided for.

52. THE CIRCLE JOINED TO STRAIGHT STEMS.—It is obvious that a straight stem has two sides to which a circle can be joined with equal facility; but to satisfy the requirements of shorthand writing, the simple circle is confined to one side of these stems, according to the following rule:

53. The small circle for S or Z is joined to straight stems with Backward Motion, as follows:

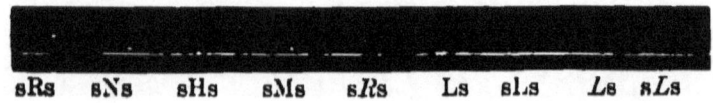

sRs　sNs　sHs　sMs　s*R*s　Ls　s*L*s　*L*s　s*L*s

The downward forms for R and L, it will be seen, are slanted less than their upward forms, and their Stenotypes are printed in italics.

54. The joining of the S circle at the beginning of L requires special mention. The following considerations

will make the scheme plain: 1st. This circle is always joined at the beginning of R with Backward Motion. 2d. The hook of L may be written on either side (Par. 9); then, to save the necessity of writing the circle carefully inside the hook of L, we can, by turning the circle with Forward Motion, include both the circle and hook, without any conflict with the R stem, with initial S circle. Observe that the downward L is commenced at the top, and consequently the hook and circle included will be found at the top. At the end of L the circle is governed by the same rule as is applied to the other straight stems, being joined with Backward Motion.

NOTE 36.—When any circle, loop, or hook is joined finally to L, the straightness of the stem will be preserved by writing the initial hook on the opposite side from the circle, loop or hook, as shown in the Plate.

55. The sound of N is represented by a medium-sized circle joined to stems at either end, and read in the order in which it is written. It is turned on the inside of curves, as follows:

nTn   nJn   nKn   nThn   Bn   Fn   Shn   Sn

It is joined initially to straight stems with Backward Motion, and finally with Forward or Backward Motion, according to convenience, as follows:

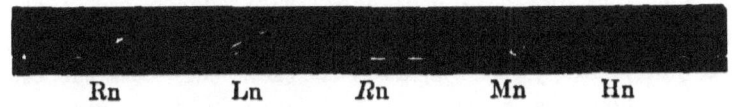

Rn   Ln   Ṛn   Mn   Hn

The Stenotype of this circle is the small or lower-case n.

NOTE 37.—It will be found more convenient to join the N circle finally with Backward Motion to all straight stems except downward R and H, where Forward Motion will be more convenient.

LESSON XII.

VOCALIZATION OF STEMS WITH CIRCLES ATTACHED.

(Illustrated by the Plate on page 190.)

56. Vowels occurring between the sound represented by the S circle and the sound of the stem to which it is attached, are pointed in instead of joined, being written on the proper side of the stem. This circle at the beginning of a stem always reads first.

LINE 12.—Sip, sad, such, sky, sir, sly, snow, sing.

NOTE 38.—Vowels occurring after a stem having an initial circle may be joined when convenient.

EXAMPLES.—Sap, sop. spy, soap, sup, soup, spew, sob, sty, stay, stow, city, stew, sod, soda, seed, seedy, side, sage, sedge, siege, sack, sock, sky, scow, Psyche, sake, soak, suck, seek, sick, skew, sag, soggy, south, scythe, soothe, sash, saucy, Susie, sere, sewer, sour, sill, silly, seal, slaw, slay, sleigh, Saul, slow, slew, soil, seem, same, psalm, some, sung, sang, sway, soho.

57. This circle at the end of a stem always reads last.

LINE 13.—Peace, adz, chess, geese, race, lose, miss, use.

NOTE 39.—Vowels occurring before a stem having a final circle may be joined when convenient.

EXAMPLES.—Peas, pace, pass, paws, pause, pose, puss, pus, pies, apes, bees, baize, bays, bass, base, boss, buys, boys, bows, boughs, ebbs, abyss, abase, obeys, abbess, abuse, abbeys, tease, toss, toes, ties, toys, adds, dies, dice, days, does, dues, deuce, adduce, cheese, chase, chaws, chose, choose, chews, choice, itches, etches, ægis, ages, edges, jaws, juice, Jews, joys, keys, kiss, ekes, case, aches, Cass, axe, cause, ox, oaks, echoes, coos, accuse, cows, gaze, guess, eggs, gas, gauze, goes, goose, guise, fees, phiz, face, efface, fuse, effuse, office, foes, fuss eaves, vase, views, vice, vies, voice, vows, avows, thaws, thews, thighs, this, those, thus, ears, rays, arrows, arose, rose, rows, ruse, rice, rouse, arouse, lees, lace, lays, lass, less, loss, loose, lice, lies, alas, louse, allows, niece, knees, inns, gnaws, nose, noose, nice, noise, ounce, amiss, mace, maize, amaze, aims, miss, mass, amass, alms, moss, moose, muse, amuse, mice, mouse, ways, woes, woos, yes, ewes, yews, hiss, haze, Hayes, hose, hoes, hies, house.

58. When a stem has a circle at each end the vowels belonging to it are best pointed in.

LINE 14.—Spice, seeds, sages, sails, psalms, Swiss.

EXAMPLES.—Sips, space, sops, soaps, suppose, spews, soups, spies, spouse, sobs, cities, stays, stows, stews.

59. Stems with the N circle attached are vocalized in the same manner as those with the S circle (Pars. 56-58).

NOTE 40.—This circle, like the S circle, reads first when joined at the beginning, and last when at the end of a stem.

LINE 15.—Knotty, nudge, neck, tin, run, men, yon, hone.

EXAMPLES.—Natty, notch, niche, knack, knock, nook, nag, nog, 'neath, pin, pain, pane, pen, pan, pawn, pun, pine, been, bean, bane, Ben, ban, bone, bun, boon, attain, ten, tan, tone, atone, ton, tine, town, Dean, Eden, din, dawn, Dane, Dan, den, deign, don, done, dine, chin, chain, chine, gin, Jane, John, June, join, keen, kin, akin, cane, ken, can (noun), con, cone, coon, kine, coin, gain, again, gone, gun, gown, fin, fain, feign, fen, fan, fawn, often, fun, fine, vain, vane, van, Vaughan, vine, thin, then, thine, sheen, shin, ashen, shone, shown, shun, ocean, shine, seen, sane, sawn, sown, sun, son, zone, rain, reign, wren, ran, roan, run, Rhine, mean, main, mane, men, amen, man, moan, omen, moon, mine, yawn, hen, Hun.

60. The outlines of a great many words, beginning with a vowel, with N as the first consonant sound, may be shortened materially, without sacrificing legibility, by using the N circle to represent that sound. Then, to show that the vowel comes before the n, it may be conventionally written inside the circle.

NOTE 41.—In practice it is seldom necessary to insert this vowel.

LINE 16.—Into, unto, undo, inch, enjoy, Inca.

LESSON XIII.

CIRCLES BETWEEN STEMS.—CIRCLES FOLLOWING OTHER CIRCLES.

(Illustrated by the Plate on page 190.)

61. When a circle occurs between two stems, if the stems join at an angle the circle is turned on the outside of that angle, and if the stems do not join at an angle, the circle is turned on that side of the first stem which it would occupy if no stem followed it.

LINE 17.—Chesapeake, fasten, reason, desk, museum, poison.

(The remainder of this lesson is illustrated by the Plate on page 191.)

LINE 1.—Panama, bench, tenor, candy, fancy, runaway.

EXAMPLES.—(These words are all of two stems with the S circle between).—Tacit, phthisic, task, tusk, Tuesday, tossing, teasing, deceit, deceive, disk, disavow, dismay, dosing, dusky, dowsing, chasten, Atchison, chosen, choosing, Jason, Joseph, accede, exit, cask, cassock, chasm, oxide, Cossack, oxen, causing, gazing, guessing, gassing, gasp, Augusta, gossip, gusset, physic, facade, facing, effacing, fusing, visage, season, schism, paucity, opposite, opacity, pasty, upset, episode, passage, passeth (*P*), possess (*P*), pacify, passing, pausing, pacing, posing, opposing, appeasing, opossum, bask, Biscay, besought, beset, bestow, obesity, beside, beseech, besiege, abusive, basing, boatswain, bassoon, besom, nicer (*R*), answer (*R*), noisome, Anson, unsung, mask, mosque, Moscow, music, musk, missive, massive, misery (R), miser (*R*), mouser (*R*), mizzen, mason, wisp, wasp, Wesson, yeasty, user (*R*), usury, hasp, hasty, husk, hasten.

(These words are all of two stems with the N circle between).—Bandy, banner, tanner, tannery, dainty, dinner, January, junior, cannery, gainer, gunner, finer, finery, shiner, runner (RnR), minute, Monday, month, miner, meaning, handy, haunch, Henry, honing.

62. The rule given in Par. 61 is departed from only to

avoid turning a circle on the back of a curved stem; circles must always be turned on the inside of curves.

LINE 2.—Risk, nosegay, message, ranch, launch, manage.

NOTE 42.—The stem L may be used for initial L when followed by a circle and another stem, as in "launch," in Line 2.

EXAMPLES.—Reside, lucid, Lusk, range, linnet, lunch, lounge, munch.

63. Another S sound may be added after an S circle at the end of a word by turning a small circle on the back of the S circle, and after an N circle by turning a small circle inside the N circle. The Stenotype remains s.

LINE 3.—Pieces, doses, races, laces, fans, signs, runs, moons.

NOTE 43.—On straight stems the first circle is turned with Backward Motion, according to rule, and the following S circle is turned on the back of the first by carrying the pencil across the stem and half way round the first circle, where the lines join, forming the "divided circle." The N circle is turned in its proper direction, and the S circle is turned inside of it by continuing the circular motion of the pencil until it forms a complete small circle inside of the larger one, presenting the "inclosed circle."

NOTE 44.—The obscure vowel occurring between the two S sounds may be left unrepresented.

EXAMPLES.—(*Small circle on the back of the S circle*).—Paces, passes, pauses, poses, opposes, bases, bosses, buzzes, teases, tosses, dazes, adzes, dowses, cheeses, chases, chooses, Jesus, cases, axes, causes, cusses, gazes, guesses, gases, fizzes, phases, faces, fusses, vases, offices, fuses, vices, voices, ceases, assesses, sauces, sowses, roses, rises, arises (*R*ss), rouses, arouses, leases, losses, loses, looses, neices, noses, nooses, noises, misses, mazes, maces, amazes, messes, masses, mosses, musses, muses, amuses, uses, hisses, houses.

(*Small circle within the N circle*).—Pins, pains, pens, pans, pawns, puns, pines, beans, bins, bans, bones, buns, boons, tins, tens, tans, tones, tons, tines, towns, Deans, dins, dens, Dan's, dawns, dines, downs, chins, chains, chance, chines, jeans, gins, Jane's, Jones, joins, canes, cans, cones, coons, coins, gains, gowns, fins, fens, feigns, fawns, evince, vanes, vans, vines, shins, shuns, shines, rains, means, mince, manes, mains, men's, man's, moans, mines, Haines, hens, hence, hones, Huns.

64. Two S sounds following the N circle are represented by elongating the small circle into a loop and turning it on the back of the N circle. The Stenotype of this loop is ss.

LINE 4.—Pounces, dunces, chances, Kansas, fences, rinses.

EXAMPLES.—Bounces, tenses, dances, Jones's, offences (*F*), evinces, minces.

65. The N circle may be used for M in a few special cases where there is no danger of conflict between N and M, the circle being made larger than usual for M when convenient. The Stenotype of the circle when used for M is the small or lower-case m.

LINE 5.—Money, pomp, submit, item, damp, Smith, name.

EXAMPLES.—Pampa, Pompey, pump, bump, bumper (Bm*PR*), Autumn, damper, dump, camp, gimp, many, smooth (Sm*Dh*), hamper (Hm*PR*), hump.

LESSON XIV.

REPRESENTATION OF S AND Z.

(Illustrated by the Plate on page 191.)

66. When Z is the first consonant in a word (preceded or not by a vowel) it must be represented by the stem Zee.

LINE 6.—Zero, zinc, Ezra, Zion, Zurich, oozing, zany.

NOTE 45.—The connecting hook should of course be used when necessary to secure a distinct angle in joining.

EXAMPLES.—Czar, Isaac, Zachariah, Zebedee.

67. When Z is the last consonant in a word, *and is followed by a vowel*, the stem Zee must be used.

LINE 7.—Busy, cozy, fuzzy, rosy, noisy, Maza.

EXAMPLES.—Posy, boozy, dizzy, daisy, dozy, Josie, fuzee, Vesey, uneasy, mazy.

68. When S is the first consonant in a word, *and is preceded by a vowel*, it must be represented by the stem Ess.

LINE 8.—Ask, asp, askew, ossify, Essex, Eason, isthmus.

EXAMPLES.—Æsop, Esquimaux, escape, espy, Osage, Estey.

69. When S is the last consonant in a word, *and is followed by a vowel*, the stem Ess must be used.

LINE 9.—Posse, Jessie, fussy, Vasa, racy, Massa.

EXAMPLES.—Abbacy, Tasso, Odyssey, Odessa, Jesse, juicy, Agassiz, foci, Macy, massy.

70. When not governed by the foregoing rules, the sounds of S and Z should be represented by the stems Ess and Zee respectively, when the stems will clearly give an easier form than would result from the use of the circle s.

LINE 10.—Suffice, excess, Smith, smooth, exercise, season, Cicero, Cæsar.

71. When a word contains but the two consonants, S followed by S or Z, use one stem and one circle, as follows: When the word ends in S or Z, no vowel following, use the stem followed by the circle; when a vowel follows the last S or Z, use the circle followed by the stem.

LINE 11.—Cease, says, sauce, size, sissy, saucy.

EXAMPLES.—Sees, seize, siss, sows, sues, sighs, Susie.

72. In all cases not governed by Pars. 66, 67, 68, 69, 70, and 71, the small circle s should be used for S and Z. (See Lesson XI.)

LESSON XV.

LOOPS FOR STR, TR (DR, THR, DHR), AND SHN.

(Illustrated by Plate on page 191.)

73. A small loop, written *only at the beginning of stems*, is used for the combination str, with no vowel between the three consonants. It is joined to stems in the same manner as the S circle (inside of curves, and to straight stems with Backward Motion). Its Stenotype is str in lower-case letters.

LINE 12.—Strip, straight, stretch, strike, strive, stress, stroll, strain, string.

NOTE 46.—This loop is joined to L on the same principle as the S circle. (See Par. 54.)

EXAMPLES.—Strap, street, strait, strut, strode, stride, streak, stroke, struck, strife, Strine, stream, strong.

74. A small loop, less than half the length of a short stem, *used only at the end of stems*, represents tr, dr, or dhr, an obscure vowel, which may be left unrepresented, occurring between the r and the preceding consonant. It is turned within curves and joined to straight stems with Forward Motion. Its Stenotype is tr in lower-case letters.

LINE 13.—Better, tighter, daughter, gather, fetter, Astor, lighter, enter.

EXAMPLES.—Patter, Potter, pouter, powder, beater, bitter, bidder, batter, bother, butter, biter, teeter, titter, tetter, tatter, totter, auditor, debtor, doubter, cutter, gaiter, getter, gutter, goitre, fitter, fighter, avator, shatter, shutter, shooter, shouter, sitter, setter, Sutter, ratter, rooter, litter, loiter, neater, knitter, mutter, miter, heater, hatter, hater, hotter, header.

75. The tr loop may follow any circle, in the manner here shown, after the stems P and B only.

LINE 14.—Paster, pester, pastor, poster, painter, pander, pointer, boaster, booster, banter, binder.

NOTE 47.—The tr loop in this situation cannot conveniently be used on other stems. The method of writing other words with similar terminations will be explained hereafter.

76. A large loop, more than half the length of a short stem, *used only at the end of stems*, represents the syllable "shon," spelled variously "tion," "sion," "cian," etc. It is turned within curves, and joined to straight stems with Backward Motion. Its Stenotype is shn in lower-case letters.

LINE 15.—Passion, occasion, vision, lesion, appellation, vocation, discussion, exception.

EXAMPLES.—Option, potion, edition, action, caution, auction, fashion, fusion, effusion, evasion, vacation, session, ration, oration (*R*shn), erasion, erosion, elision (*L*shn), elation, lotion, illusion, allusion, notion, motion, mission, emission, omission, emotion, unction, Hessian. (*Two stems ending with shon loop*.)—Pollution (P*L*shn), aberration, abortion, adoption, diction, division, diffusion, adoration, dilation, dilution, adhesion (D*c*Hshn), Egyptian, agitation, ejection, caption, corrosion, cohesion (K*c*Hshn), gumption, ignition, fiction, faction, Phœnician (*F*Nshn), eviction, vacation, avocation, variation (V*R*shn), association (SShshn), eruption (*R*Pshn), irritation, irradiation, erection, irrigation, arrogation, refashion, revision, remission, election, allegation, elevation, alleviation, alienation, infusion, invasion, animation.

77. S or Z is added to a loop by turning the small circle on the back of the stem.

LINE 16.—Patters, fetters, pastors, binders, auctions, rations, alienations.

78. When two vowels occur together, as in "alienations," the last word in Line 16, when one of the vowels is the dot

e, it may be represented, for convenience of joining, by its mate A.

EXAMPLES.—(Select from the words given under Pars. 74, 75, and 76, adding the S circle to them.)

79. The shon loop may include any circle, any vowel occurring between the circle and loop being omitted or written inside the loop.

LINE 17.—Opposition, decision, disposition, tension, redemption.

NOTE 48.—The vowel between the circle and loop above mentioned is seldom or never required to be written, the form being perfectly legible without it.

EXAMPLES.—Position, apposition, supposition, deposition, admission, indisposition (nDsPsshn), exposition, accusation, vexation.

LESSON XVI.

INITIAL HOOKS.

(Illustrated by the Plate on page 192.)

80. The sounds of R and L unite very closely with other consonant sounds, the combination being uttered by one impulse of the voice. In such words as "pray," "try," "clay," "fly," etc., it will be noticed that "pr," "tr," "cl," and "fl," in those words are so closely united as to appear to be but one sound, no vowel occurring between them. This combination of R and L with other sounds is represented by an adequately close and rapid combination of forms.

81. The sound of R *following* the sound of a stem is indicated by a small hook at the *beginning* of stems written

within curves, and joined to straight stems by Forward Motion, as follows:

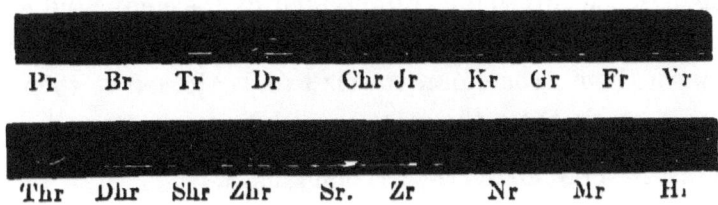

The Stenotype of this hook is the small or lower-case r.

NOTE 49.—Although written *first* in forming the outline, this R hook sounds *after* the stem to which it is attached. The first outline in the table above is "Pr," not "rP"; R before another consonant being always represented by the stem Ar.

82. R and L do not take the R hook. The wave signs Ng, W, and Y do not take it except in certain special forms when connected with a preceding stem, as shown in the Vocabulary.

83. The sound of L *following* the sound of a stem is indicated, on curves, by a *large* hook at the *beginning* of stems, and on straight stems by a *small* hook at the *beginning*, turned with Backward Motion, as follows:

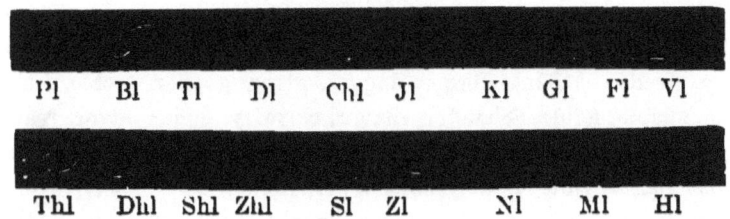

The Stenotype of this hook is the small or lower-case l.

NOTE 50.—Although written first, as in the case of the R hook, this hook sounds after the stem to which it is attached.

84. R and L do not take the L hook. The wave signs Ng, W, and Y do not take it except in certain cases when following other stems, as shown in the Vocabulary.

85. These initially hooked stems are compound stems, and are vocalized, joined, and read the same as simple stems—that is, the two sounds represented by the compound stem are spoken with one impulse and with no vowel sound between them; therefore, vowels will be joined to them or written beside them the same as with simple stems.

LINE 1.—Pray, draw, acre, fry, throw, inner.

EXAMPLES.—Pry, prow, bray, brew, brow, tree, tray, trow, true, try, Tray, dray, drew, dry, crow, crew, cry, eager, gray, augur, grow, agree, free, fray, affray, offer, fro, Ophir, over, three, author, threw, either, Asher, usher, shrew, honor, owner, Emir.

LINE 2.—Blow, idle, clue, evil, easel, inly, only.

EXAMPLES.—Plea, play, ply, plow, able, blue, blew, addle, idly, clay, claw, cloy, glee, eagle, glow, ogle, glue, flee, flea, flay, flow, flew, fly.

86. These hooks are used between stems as well as at the beginning of words.

LINE 3.—Tucker, trifle, chiefly, shovel, ripple, rifle, roamer.

NOTE 51.—The slight vowel heard between the stem and hook in such words as "Tucker," "shovel," "roamer," need not be represented.

EXAMPLES.—Teacher, tickle, taker, tackle, talker, travel, trimmer, decry, decline (DKln), digger, dagger, giver, gopher, feeble, feebly, fable, affable, foible, Schaeffer, shaver, chivalry, suffer, savor, reaper, ripper, Ripley, wrapper, roper, reply, rabble, rubber, ruble, richer, richly, rigger, riffle, raffle, ruffle, leper, lubber, labor, ledger, lodger, liquor, locker, lugger, liver, lover, lovely, lively, muckle, maker, mocker, mockery, muffle (MFl), heifer (HFr), homely.

NOTE 52.—Use the stem El for initial L in such words as "leper," "lubber," "labor," given in the above exercise.

87. Sometimes the hook can only be partially written; in such cases a slight offset of the pencil answers the purpose.

LINE 4.—Paper, table, trouble, finely, neighbor, employ, hammer.

EXAMPLES.—Tipple, taper, topple, toper, deeper, dipper, dapper, dapple, doubly, double, feather, razor, nipple, noble, nobly, enable, unable, ennoble, masher, Mosher, haggle.

88. In some cases it is better to write the stems instead of trying to use the hooks, when the latter cannot well be shown.

LINE 5.—Pauper, trapper, trooper, joker, cracker, shipper.

LESSON XVII.

REVERSED L HOOK.

(Illustrated by the Plate on page 192.)

89. The large L hook, as shown on curves, is frequently reversed and joined at an angle to stems at either end to represent an initial or final L sound. At the beginning of words it always opens up or down, and at the end of words it takes the most convenient direction. It is read in the order in which it is written. It should be a half-circle, twice the size of the vowel u—that is, one-sixteenth of an inch in diameter. Its Stenotype is the small lower-case *l* printed in italics.

NOTE 53.—A small (u) or (d) in parenthesis printed after the Stenotype of this hook indicates the direction toward which it should open in a given outline, whether up or down.

LINE 6.—Leap, latch, lug, leaf, loathe, lash, line, limb.

LINE 7.—Bull, tail, chill, goal, fill, rule, lull, mile, Yale, hill.

EXAMPLES.—(*One stem preceded by reversed L hook*).—Lip, lap, lop, loop, lench, liege, ledge, leek, leak, lick, lake, lack, lock, luck, look, like, leg, lag, log, laugh, loaf, luff, leave, lave, latch, loth, lathe, lithe, leash, lash, lean, lane, lawn, lone, loon, loin, lame, lamb, loam, loom, lime, Lang.

(*One stem with reversed L hook at the end*).—Peel, pill, pale, poll, pole, pool, pull, pile, bill, bale, ball, bawl, bowl, bile, boil, teal, tall, toll, tool, tile, toil, deal, dale, dell, doll, dole, dull, gill, gaol, jail, jowl, keel, kill, call, coal, cull, cool, chyle, coil, cowl, gale, gall, guile, feel, fail, fell, fall, fool, file, foil, foul, fowl, veal, vale, vile, thole, reel, rill, rail, roll, loll, meal, mill, male, mail, maul, mole, mule, yell, yawl, heel, hale, hell, hall, haul, hole, whole, hull.

NOTE 54.—The reversed L hook, as shown in the above examples, is almost always used to represent initial L followed by a stem, and final L preceded by a stem. The only exceptions to this practice are in words like "labor" or "Laura," where L is best represented by the stem El, and "excel" (Ks*L*), where the stem L must be used to admit of vocalization if desirable. L at the beginning of words and preceded by a vowel, and L at the end of words and followed by a vowel, are always represented by the stem El, to admit of vocalization if necessary.

90. The S circle only can be written inside the reversed L hook. No other circle or loop is allowable.

LINE 8.—Sleep, slouch, slack, slim, sling, pulse, tails, rolls, heels.

EXAMPLES—Slip, slap, slop, slope, sloop, slab, sledge, sleek, slick, slake, slag, slug, sloth, slash, slush, slam, slime, slung, slang. (For S added to the reversed L hook at the end of words, use the words given under Par. 89, Line 7.)

91. The combination "sl" at the end of a word, sometimes with a slight vowel, which may be left unrepresented, intervening between the two sounds, is also represented by the reversed L hook preceded by the S circle. The circle is joined to straight stems with Backward Motion, according to Par. 53, the hook following in the most convenient direction.

LINE 9.—Pestle, dazzle, jostle, fizzle, rustle, nozzle, hustle.

EXAMPLES.—Puzzle, bustle, tassel, tussle, chisel, castle, guzzle, vessel, vassal, thistle, sizzle, wrestle, nasal, missile, muzzle, weasel, wassail, hazel.

92. Another s may be turned inside the reversed L hook, as used in Par. 91.

LINE 10.—Pestles, dazzles, jostles, fizzles, rustles, nozzles, hustles.

EXAMPLES.—(Use the words given under Par. 91.)

LESSON XVIII.

CIRCLES AND THE STR LOOP ATTACHED TO INITIAL HOOKS.—SPECIAL VOCALIZATION.

(Illustrated by the Plate on page 192.)

93. The S circle is the only circle prefixed to compound curved stems. It is turned inside the hook. The str loop is not allowable in this situation.

LINE 11.—Spry, sprawl, stray, scrawl, screech, scream.

EXAMPLES.—Spree, spray, straw, strew, scrip, scrape, scrap, scrub, scribe, scratch, scraggy, scroll, screw, screen (sKrn), scrawny (sKrN).

94. The str loop or any circle may be prefixed to a compound R hook straight stem by turning the loop or circle with Forward Motion, the hook being included in the circle. It will be remembered that the simple circles and loop are joined to straight stems with Backward Motion. (See Pars. 53 and 55.)

LINE 12.—Sinner, simmer, summer, manner, strainer, streamer.

95. When the S circle occurs between a compound stem and a preceding stem, when practicable both the circle and hook must be shown. In the case of two straight stems in the same direction, it is sufficient to turn the circle with Forward Motion for the R hook. No circle or loop except the S circle can be used in this situation.

LINE 13.—(First three words.)—Display, house-fly, Messmer.

96. When not conveniently formed, the hook may be omitted following the circle between stems, or the sound of the hook may be represented by the proper stem.

LINE 13.—(Last three words.)—Describe, disagree, Jasper.

97. It is sometimes convenient to use a compound stem when its sounds do not closely unite—that is, when a distinct vowel occurs between them; then, to represent the vowel as coming between the sound of the stem and that of the hook, the vowel should be struck *through* the stem. The vowels A and o may be varied slightly from the horizontal and vertical to accomplish this when necessary. may be represented by its mate A for this purpose.

LINE 14.—Power, tell, cheer, fellow, violet, entire, here.

EXAMPLES.—Pure, till, delight (DlT), cheerful, chair, char, chore, agile, July, joyful, care, careful, follow, full, fully, village (*Vl*J), virtue (*V*rCh), vulture (*V*lChR), sheer, shale, share, shawl, shore, sure, azure, sell, easily, soul, repair, rebel, retire, recall, recur, regal, regale, rueful, reveal, ravel, revel, reamer, rammer, label (LBl), lappel, libel, until, endear, endure, nature (NChr), nurture (NrChr), angel, incur, sinecure (sNKr), naval, novel, Mitchell, hovel.

LESSON XIX.

EXCEPTIONAL HOOKS.

(Illustrated by the Plate on page 192.)

98. When W is the first sound in a word consisting of more than one consonant sound, it may be represented by a small half-circle, joined to the following stem at the most acute angle, and opening to the right or left. It is the same size as the vowel u—one thirty-second of an inch

across. Its Stenotype is the small or lower-case *w* printed in italics.

NOTE 55.—A small (r) or (l) in parenthesis, printed after the Stenotype of this half-circle, indicates the direction toward which it should open in a given outline, whether to the right or left.

LINE 15.—Weep, weapon, wits, wedge, wax, wife, wafer, wash, war.

EXAMPLES.—Web, wait, wet, weed, widow, wade, wed, wide, witch, watch, wage, week, weak, walk, woke, wig, wag, waif, woof, weave, wave, waver, wove, wives, withe, wither, weather, wisher (*w*Sh*R*), weary (*w*R), wary, wear, wore, wire, wing.

99. This W half-circle may also be prefixed to any vowel, or used medially between stems, or between consonants and vowels.

LINE 16.—Quip, thwack, quake, quaff, query, squaw.

NOTE 56.—When pointed in, it is generally sufficient to simply write the half-circle in the place of the vowel, omitting the latter.

EXAMPLES—(*w joined medially*).—Quota, quack, quoth, squeak, quiver, quaver, squeal, quarry, squall, squeeze (sK*w*s). (*w pointed in*)—Quick, queer, Squib, squab, squabble.

100. The L hook (see Par. 83) may be exceptionally used for W in the words here referred to, and in cases analogous where this hook will greatly improve the outline of the word. The Stenotype of the hook used for this purpose remains unchanged, being the lower-case l.

LINE 17.—Twitch, tweak, twig, twice, quill, quail.

(The remainder of this lesson is illustrated by the Plate on page 193.)

101. The sound of W following the sound of H may be indicated by a large initial hook joined to the left side of that stem. In analogy with the R and L hooks, though formed *before*, it is pronounced *after* the stem to which it is attached. Its Stenotype is a lower-case w.

Line 1.—Whoa, why, whip, whack, whig, whisper, whiskey, whistle, wheel, whence, whine, whim.

102. The sound of W *preceding* the sound of L, N, or M, may be indicated by a large initial hook joined on the most convenient side. The most convenient side will be the left side of L (upward or downward form), the left side of M, and the upper side of N. This hook differs from any other initial hook in that it reads *before* the stem to which it is attached—that is, it reads in the order in which it is written. It is joined to L by simply enlarging the hook which L already has. The Stenotype of this hook is the small or lower-case w.

Line 2.—Weal, wool, Walter, willow, William, one, wine, Wednesday, wimble.

Note 57.—Use the upward form of L when a vowel follows the stem, as in the word "willow," in Line 2.

Examples.—Wail, well, wall, wile, wallow, Willett (w*L*T), wallet, Woolwich, Welch, welkin (w*L*Kn), wolverine (w*L V*rn), wealth (w*L*Th), wealthy, Welsh (wLSh), walrus, woolen (w*L*N), Walling, wean, win, winner, wen, wan, won, winter, windy, window, winch, wench, once, wince, winsome, winnow, women (wMn), woman, Wemple, wampum (wMPM).

LESSON XX.

FINAL HOOKS.

(Illustrated by the Plate on page 193.)

103. The sounds of T, D, F, and V following other stems occur so frequently that, if written with their alphabetic forms in all cases, they would render the execution of the writing too slow for verbatim work. The use of the stems in all cases would also give rise to very awkward forms

seriously detrimental to speed. To provide adequately for the representation of these frequently recurring sounds, they are indicated by final hooks attached to all stems, and read in the order in which they are written.

104. The sound of T or D is represented by a *small* hook written *at the end of stems*. It is turned on the inside of curves, and joined to straight stems with Forward Motion for the sound of T, and Backward Motion for the sound of D, as follows:

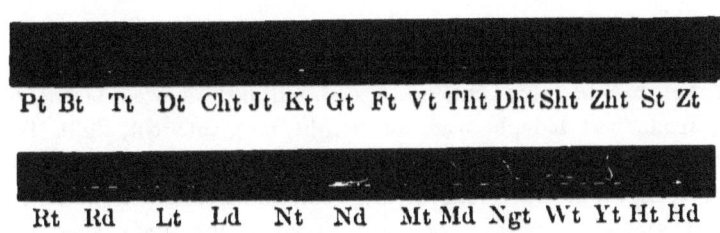

Pt Bt Tt Dt Cht Jt Kt Gt Ft Vt Tht Dht Sht Zht St Zt

Rt Rd Lt Ld Nt Nd Mt Md Ngt Wt Yt Ht Hd

The Stenotype of this hook on curves is the small or lower-case t; on straight stems its Stenotype is the lower-case t when turned with Forward Motion, and the lower-case d when turned with Backward Motion. It is called the T hook.

105. The sound of F or V is represented by a *large* hook written *at the end of stems*, and joined in the same manner as the T hook. On straight stems it is turned with Forward Motion for F, and Backward Motion for V, as follows:

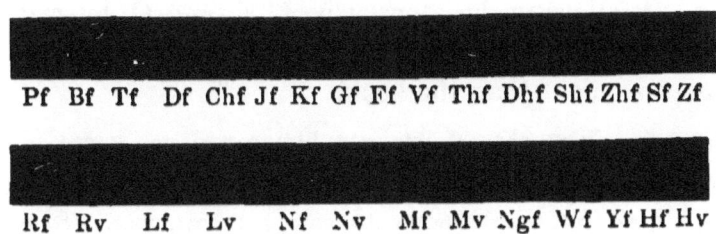

Pf Bf Tf Df Chf Jf Kf Gf Ff Vf Thf Dhf Shf Zhf Sf Zf

Rf Rv Lf Lv Nf Nv Mf Mv Ngf Wf Yf Hf Hv

The Stenotype of this hook on curves is the small or lower-case f; on straight stems its Stenotype is the lower-case f when turned with Forward Motion, and the lower-case v when turned with Backward Motion. It is called the F hook.

106. Vowels are joined or written beside stems with these final hooks the same as in the case of the stems alone.

LINE 3.—Peat, apt, deed, fate, thought, showed, set, eased, write, read, note, end.

EXAMPLES.—(*Single stems followed by the T hook*).—Pit, pate, paid, aped, pat, pet, pad, pot, pawed, pod, pied, pout, beat, bit, bate, bait, bet, bot, bought, boat, boot, bead, bid, bode, bowed, bayed, bed, bad, abode, bud, bide, buoyed, tat, taught, tote, tut, toot, tight, Todd, towed, tide, tied, toyed, date, dot, dote, doubt, deed, dead, added, died, feet, fit, fat, aft, fought, oft, foot, fight, vat, vote, vied, void, vowed, viewed, thawed, shot, shut, shoot, shout, shade, shed, shad, shod, scat, sit, sate, sat, sought, sot, soot, sight, site, cite, oozed, writ, rat, rot, wrought, rote, wrote, root, rout, rid, read, red, rod, rowed, rood, rued, neat, knit, net, gnat, ant, not, nut, night, knout, need, nod, gnawed, node, owned, annoyed, weighed, wooed.

LINE 4.—Puff, dove, chafe, calf, five, thief, shave, seive, reef, rave, enough, knave.

EXAMPLES.—(*Single stems followed by the F hook*).—Pave, beef, buff, above, tough, deaf, doff, chief, chaff, achieve, Jove, gyve, cough, cuff, cave, cove, gaff, Gough, gave, sheaf, sheave, shove, safe, save, salve, rough, roof, rife, reave (Rv), rove, rive, knife.

107. A distinction may be made between the sounds of T and D following the stems Ch, J, K, and G, by writing T with the stem and D with the hook, the stem being rather more convenient than the hook.

LINE 5.—Cheat, chewed, jet, aged, kite, cowed, get, guyed.

EXAMPLES (*Two stems*).—Chit, chat, etched, Choate, jot, jut, jute, eked, kit, cat, cot, caught, cut, cute, gate, got, goat, gout. (*Stem fol-*

lowed by the T hook.)—Chid, chawed, chide, jade, edged, jawed, joyed, Jude, keyed, kid, cawed, cud, cooed, gad.

108. To avoid the inconvenience of the backward hook for T on the stems M and H, represent T by the stem, D being represented by the proper hook. F and V may both be represented by the Backward Motion hook on these stems for the same reason.

LINE 6.—Meat, made, hit, hid, muff, move, half, heave.

EXAMPLES (*Two stems*).—Mit, mate, met, mat, mote, mite, might, heat, hate, hat, hot, hut, hoot, height, Hoyt. (*Stem followed by the D hook.*)—Mead, mud, amid, aimed, maid, mad, Maud, mode, mowed, mud, mood, mewed, heed, head, had, hod, hoed, hood, hide. (*Stem with V hook.*)—Miff, huff, hoof, halve, hove, hive.

NOTE 58.—By a judicious use of the hooks explained in this lesson contrasted with the stem signs for the same sounds, great increase of legibility may be attained. The hooks may be used when the sound they represent is the last sound in the word, and the stem signs when that sound is followed by a vowel. This principle will be more fully amplified hereafter.

LESSON XXI.

CIRCLE AND HOOK FOLLOWING HOOKS.—T TICK.

(Illustrated by the Plate on page 193.)

109. The S circle is the only circle added to final hooks. On curved stems it is always turned inside the hook.

LINE 7.—Pets, debts, chiefs, coves, thieves, sheaves, safes.

EXAMPLES.—(Use the words given under Par. 106, Lines 3 and 4.)

110. On straight stems the S circle may be added to a T hook by turning the circle with Forward Motion, the hook being included in the circle. It will be remembered that the simple circle is joined to straights with Backward Motion. (See Par. 53.) This principle is in analogy with

that explained in Par. 94 concerning the circle and R hook. To the D hook, and the F hook on straight stems, the circle is added by turning it inside the hook.

Line 8.—Writes, reads, lights, loads, notes, nodes, moods, heads, reefs, raves, knives, moves, heaves.

Examples.—(Use the words given under Par. 106, Lines 3 and 4.)

111. The sound of T or D, following the sound of any hook, may be represented as follows: After the F hook, or reversed L hook, by turning the T hook within the first hook; after a T or D hook by a short, slanting tick, called the "T tick," joined at an angle. The past tense of verbs ending in *ed* as a separate syllable is represented by this T tick when the present tense ends in a T hook. The Stenotype of this T tick is a lower-case *t* printed in italics.

Line 9.—Paved, achieved, cuffed, thefts, shafts, soft, raved, miffed, heft.

Examples.—(Use the words given under Par. 106, Line 4.)

Line 10.—Peeled, dolt, jilts, felt, rolled, lulled, mild, mold.

Examples.—(Use the words given under Par. 89, Line 7.)

Line 11.—Dated, goaded, shotted, suited, rated, loaded, netted, headed.

Examples.—(Use the words given under Par. 106, Line 3.)

LESSON XXII.

SHON LOOP, REVERSED L HOOK, AND VOWELS FOLLOWING THE T HOOK.—T HOOK FOLLOWING CIRCLES AND LOOPS.—HOOKED VOWELS.

(Illustrated by the Plate on page 193.)

112. The shon loop, or the reversed L hook, may follow the T hook in the manner here indicated, the vowel occur-

ring between the hook and shon loop being omitted, or written inside the loop.

LINE 12.—Potation, disputation, rotation, battle, victuals, rattled, noddle, metal, huddle.

EXAMPLES.—Citation, notation, paddle, puddle, poodle, bottle, tittle, tattle, toddle, Toodles, kettle (Ktl), cattle, coddle, cuddle, fiddle, settle, saddle, sidle, riddle, ladle, nettle, noodle, middle, mettle, medal, mottle, model.

113. A T or D sound following a circle or loop, may be represented by adding the T hook after such circle or loop. The Stenotype of this hook in this situation remains unchanged, being the lower-case t.

LINE 13.—Post, lost, amazed, dint, lent, named, battered, muttered, occasioned, motioned, toughest.

EXAMPLES.—(*S circle followed by the T hook.*)—Pieced, appeased, paced, past, passed, paused, opposed, beast, based, abased, best, abused, teased, test, attest, tossed, dozed, chased, chest, jest, jist, just, adjust, joist, kissed, Kast, cost, coast, accused, gazed, guest, guessed, aghast, ghost, gust, feast, fist, faced, effaced, fast, fussed, foist, Faust, visit, vest, vast, ceased, assessed, soused, wrist, raced, raised, rest, roast, rust, roost, roused, aroused, least, leased, list, laced, lest, lust, loosed, mist, missed, mast, must, moist, mused, amused, wist, waste, waist, west, yeast, Yost, used, hist, hazed, host, hoist, housed, movst.

(*N circle followed by the T hook.*)—Pinned, paint, pained, pent, penned, pant, opened, pint, pined, point, pound, bent, bind, bound, tinned, taint, attained, tent, attend, tanned, toned, taunt, attuned, deigned, dent, don't, dined, chained, chant, jaunt, joint, joined, caned, Kent, canned, can't, conned, kind, coined, count, gained, gaunt, faint, feigned, fanned, font, fawned, fond, find, fined, fount, found, veined, vent, vaunt, shined, sha'n't, assent, send, signed, sound, rained, arraigned (*R*nt), rent, rant, round, lint, lend, lent, land, mint, meant, mend, amend, manned, moaned, mined, mind, mound, hint, haunt, hand, honed, hunt, hind, hound.

(*tr loop followed by the T hook.*)—Pattered, powdered, bettered, bothered, buttered, teetered, tattered, tottered, tutored, chattered, gathered, fettered, shattered, shuddered, lightered, littered, entered, mitered.

(*shn followed by the T hook.*)—Patient, cautioned, cushioned, quotient (Kshnt : *w*),* fashioned.

* NOTE 59.—When necessary to point in a vowel preceded by the sound of W, it is generally sufficient to write the half-circle *w*, omitting the vowel.

114. The circles followed by the T hook may be used between stems in words like the following. When the preceding stem is straight, the rule given in Par. 48 is applied if practicable.

LINE 14.—Chester, country, kindly, visitor, fainter, foundry, restore, arastra.

NOTE 60.—The application of the rule given in Par. 48 will be seen in the words "fainter" and "foundry," in Line 14. Either direction being equally convenient, F is so disposed as to permit the writing of R downward when no vowel follows, and upward when a vowel follows. Also in the words "restore" and "arastra," which illustrate this principle, the circle stands for simple S, being in the same relation as a circle between stems. (See Par. 61.)

EXAMPLES.—Tender, jester, gender, jointer, extra, canter, coaster, Custer, counter, gander, fester, fender, faster, foster, finder, founder, vestry (*V*stR), Ventura, thunder, sister, sender, saunter, sounder, render, roaster, rooster, Lyster, Lester, lender, laundry (Lnt*R*), luster, Nestor, mentor, muster, moister.

115. The reversed L hook, or any vowel, may follow the T hook after circles, as here shown

LINE 15.—Pedestal, crystal, bundle, kindle, fondle, mental, crusty, vista, rusty, rondo.

EXAMPLES.—Vestal, costal, spindle, brindle, trundle, dandle, gentle, candle, sandal, rental, lentil, mantle, handle, tasty, testy, dusty, audacity, gusty, frosty (Frst*i*), thirsty (Thrst*i*), lusty, nasty, nicety, honesty, misty, musty, modesty (Mtst*i*).

116. This T hook is exceptionally used before the S circle, and in connection with it, to represent the frequent com-

bination "st"—the hook, though formed before, being pronounced after the circle. Its Stenotype is st in lower-case letters. L may always be struck upward when preceded by st and standing alone, as that direction is much the more convenient, and L is scarcely ever followed by a vowel in this situation.

LINE 16.—Stop, state, stitch, stake, Stacy, store, still, stilly, stem, sting.

EXAMPLES.—Steep, step, stoop, stab, stout, steed, stead, steady, study, stood, stage, stick, sticky, stack, stalk, stock, stoke, stuck, stag, steer, star, stare, stair, stir, steel, steely, stale, stall, stole, stool, style, steam, stung.

117. The straight line vowel signs take the R, L, and T hooks.

LINE 17.—Ail (ale), awl, oar (ore), sore (soar), ire, isle (aisle), sire, odd (awed), ate, aid, owed (ode), oats.

NOTE 61.—In Line 17 the form for "ire" is struck downward, and for "isle" upward, as is evidenced by the difference in slant.

LESSON XXIII.

PREFIXES AND AFFIXES.

(Illustrated by the Plate on page 194.)

118. Owing to their frequent recurrence and the tediousness of writing them in full, certain initial syllables are provided with brief signs.

NOTE 62.—For the sake of ready illustration, words whose outlines are contracted (that is, with one or more consonant sounds unrepresented) will be occasionally made use of. Such contracted forms will be found in the Vocabulary.

119. The initial syllables *con*, *com*, and *cog* are indicated by writing a dot, called the con dot, before the beginning

of the remainder of the word. The Stenotype of this dot is a lower-case *e* printed in italics.

LINE 1.—Condone, confuse, consign, compose, combat, contrast, conceal, cognate, cognomen.

NOTE 63.—Similar syllables may occasionally be represented by the same signs, as "campaign" (*e*-Pn), but as a general rule these prefix signs should not be used for syllables which are not prefixes in the proper sense. In the word "comma," for instance, "com" not being a prefix, should not be represented by the con dot, but the word should be written in full, KM.

NOTE 64.—Vowels will be largely omitted in the exercises following, only prominent ones being written when necessary.

EXAMPLES.—Contest, concussion, connection, confusion, connive, conceit (*e*-St), concern (*e*-Srn), conciliate (*e*-s*L*T), compute, compassion, commute (*e*-YT), cognizance (*e*-NsNs).

120. When the prefix con or com occurs in the middle of a word, it may be indicated by writing the syllable which follows, near to, or if convenient, immediately under or through the syllable which precedes it. The Stenotype of this overlapping or nearness is a hyphen, and of striking through, a semicolon. In the case of vowel or tick outlines, proximity is effected by writing the vowel or tick opposite the end of the consonant stem, so as not to conflict with a "pointed in" vowel.

LINE 2.—Disconnect, recommend, circumambient, non-committal, recommence.

EXAMPLES.—Preconceived (Pr-Sft), discompose, discomfort (Ds-F*R*T), recumbent, recompense, reconnoiter, recombine, recommit, unconquered, incompetent, misconjecture.

121. nT or Nt, whichever makes the best joining, is a prefix for "enter," "inter," "intro," "ante," or "anti," joined to the rest of the word.

LINE 3.—Entertain, interdict, introduce, antidote, interjection.

122. M is a prefix for "magni," "magne," "magnan," "Mc," and "Mac," usually disjoined.

LINE 4.—Magnitude, magnetism, magnanimous, McMichael, Macdonald.

EXAMPLES.—Magnify, magnetic, magnetize, Magna Charta (M-KrT).

123. H is a prefix for "hydra," "hydro," disjoined.

LINE 5.—Hydraulic, hydrogen, hydrometry, hydrophobia, hydropical, hydrostatics.

AFFIXES.

124. The final syllable "ing" is frequently indicated by writing a dot at the end of the preceding part of the word; the plural "ings" is represented by a small circle in the same situation. The Stenotype of the dot is the lower-case *e*, and of the circle, the lower-case *s*, both printed in italics.

LINE 6.—Paying, doubting, coming, thinking, knowing, readings, cuttings.

125. The stem Ng is frequently used when it makes a good joining.

LINE 7.—Opening, being, vieing, shining, running, writing.

126. B is an affix for "ble," "bly," "bility," when Bl is not equally convenient, and Bs is an affix for "bleness." These signs are joined or disjoined according to convenience.

LINE 8.—Attainable, accountability, vendible, risible, charitableness, peaceableness, knowableness.

EXAMPLES.—Profitable, tangible, deducible, detestable, chargeable, enjoyable, accountable, forcible, insurmountable, knowable, feebleness (FBls), teachableness, questionableness (KsChnBs).

127. J is an affix for "ology," and JK for "ological," "ologically," usually disjoined, but sometimes joined in quite frequent words.

LINE 9.—Penology, biology, zoology, phraseology, physiological, theologically, etymology.

EXAMPLES.—Tautology, osteology, philology, demonology, phrenological, chronology, genealogy, geologically, doxology, astrology.

128. G, or Gr if it will join well, is an affix for "graphy," and GK or GrK for "graphic," "graphically," usually joined.

LINE 10.—Biography, Tachygraphy, Stenography, Geographic, Phonographically.

EXAMPLES.—Topography, chirography, brachygraphy, typography, orthography, calligraphy.

129. F, or f is an affix for "ful," "fully," and with Ns added, for "fulness," when those syllables cannot conveniently be written in full, usually joined.

LINE 11.—Spoonful, wrathfully, revengeful, hurtful, peacefulness, faithfulness.

EXAMPLES.—Watchfulness (*w*Ch*F*lNs), sinfulness, skillfulness, carefulness.

130. V, or f is an affix for "ever," joined.

LINE 12.—Whatever, whichever, whenever, whoever, however, wherever.

131. sV, or Sf is an affix for "soever," joined.

LINE 13—Whichsoever, whensoever, whosoever, howsoever, whithersoever, wheresoever.

132. Sh is an affix for "ship," "tial-ly," "cial-ly," usually joined.

LINE 14.—Friendship, lordship, worship, providential, deferentially, essentially, reverentially.

133. M is an affix for "ment," or "mental," when joined, and for "matic," or "matically," when disjoined.

LINE 15.—Payment, apartment, attainment, disappointment, automatic, systematically, pneumatics.

EXAMPLES.—Indictment (nDtM), resentment, firmament, ornament, sacrament, temperament (TmPM), commandment, bombardment, defacement, advancement, commencement, inducement, management, lodgment, embezzlement, abasement, disfranchisement, disbursement, abatement, excitement, achievement, movement, amazement, amusement, consignment, adornment, investment, emolument (MlM).

134. *l* is an affix for "ly" when L cannot conveniently be joined.

LINE 16.—Tightly, deadly, fitly, shortly, sightly, madly, hardly.

LESSON XXIV.

VARIOUS EXPEDIENTS.

(Illustrated by the Plate on page 195.)

135. Negative, or other words which are formed by prefixing a vowel sound to a primitive, or other derivative word, may be distinguished by prefixing the vowel sign which represents the initial vowel.

LINE 17.—Liberal, illiberal, rational, irrational, moral, immoral, memorial, immemorial.

(The remainder of this lesson is illustrated by the Plate on page 80.)

136. A proper name or an emphasized word may be noted by a dash written under it.

LINE 1.—Isaac Pitman was the founder of Phonography.

LINE 2.—So far as it is an art, it is *the* art of reasoning.

Note 65.—For contractions used, see the lists of word-signs and the Vocabulary.

137. The sound of Ng before K or G may be represented by the N circle.

Line 3.—Pink, bank, buncombe, trunk, kink, finger.

Examples.—Spunk, sprinkle, banker, bunk, bunker, bungle, tank, tinkle, drink, drunk, drunkard (DrnKRd), drank, dank, donkey, chink, chunk, jangle, junk, Jenkins (JnKns), Conkling, crank, Congo, kangaroo, gangrene, rink (RnK), rank, rankle, wrangle, wrinkle, link, lingo, lank, mink, monk, monkey, wink, Yankee, Hank, hunger, hungry (HnGR).

138. There are certain derivatives in which the name of the action and the name of the doer will differ in the shorthand outline only in the size of a loop, if written in analogy with other words, as "creation," "creator"; both being nouns, this distinction is not sufficient. To meet all such cases, use the shon loop in writing the name of the action, and the vowel eu, the name of the doer. That vowel never occurs at the end of a word, and in this situation may stand for tr.

Line 4.—Action, actor, creation, Creator, faction, factor, protection, protector.

Examples.—Let the pupil extemporize illustrations, say ten pairs of words of this character.

139. The combination "sw" is usually represented by Sl. The L hook is also used for the sound of w in the middle of words in several cases.

Line 5—(First four forms).—Switch, swab, swing, request.

Examples.—Entwine, inquest, esquire, unguent, earthquake, adequate.

140. In these four phrases the L hook is used for the sound of Y. The Stenotype remains l.

LINE 5.—(Last four forms).—By you, did you, do you, if you.

141. s is sometimes used for Sh when flexibility demands it.

LINE 6.—Objectionable, exceptionable, auctioneer, fashionable, visionary, vanquish.

142. The syllable "ed" may be added after contractions by the T tick.

LINE 7.—Regarded, recollected, perfected, effected, represented.

143. The syllables con and com may be omitted from many common words, the remainder of the word being written in the First Position.

LINE 8.—Contraction, condition, community, communion, complexion, contain.

NOTE 66.—Placing the words from which these prefixes are omitted in the First Position will prevent conflict with other words having the same forms, which generally take the other positions, as, attraction, addition, unity, union, attain.

144. "Did" must be written in full—that is, with the T hook added, when phrased with a preceding word, to prevent conflict with "do."

LINE 9.—I did not, you did, they did, how did.

145. Adapt the shorthand alphabet to the representation of initials of proper names, by writing the vowels, circle, and wave signs in the Second Position, the short stems in the First Position, and the long stems in the Third Position. Add the vowel i to G to prevent possible conflict with J.

LINES 10, 11, 12.—A, B, C, D, E, F, G, H, I, J, K, L, M, N, O, P, Q, R, S, T, U, V, W, X, Y, Z.

NOTE 67.—If written with care and with strict observance of position, the above forms will indicate the proper initial unerringly.

146. In writing numbers, use the ordinary figures, except 1, 2, 3, 4, 5, and 10, which should be written in shorthand.

Also write in shorthand, first, second, third, and fourth. Use figures for the remaining ordinal numbers; for round numbers use the contractions (see Vocabulary) for hundred, thousand, and million.

LINE 13.—One, two, three, four, five, ten, first, second, third, fourth.

LINE 14.—One thousand men reached there on the 7th day.

147. To represent a foreign sound, write the English sound nearest resembling it, and under that draw a waving dash.

LINE 15.—*Encore, Messieur, nicht, senor, Vallejo.*

148. Consonant signs which are awkward of formation in a given case, or whose sounds are obscurely heard, may frequently be omitted in order to secure a good form for a word or phrase, provided the outline remaining be suggestive.

LINE 16.—Principal-le, destruction, accomplish, excellency, extreme, gravity.

NOTE 68.—This principle will be applied freely in the lists of contractions and the Vocabulary.

149. The syllables "fication" may generally be contracted to Fshn.

LINE 17.—Purification, edification, identification, glorification, modification.

(The remainder of this lesson is illustrated by the Plate on page 196.)

150. N may often stand for "ant" or "ent" without any sacrifice of legibility.

LINE 1.—Transcendent, dependent, descendant, attendant.

151. Sh may sometimes be used for Ch, and Zh for J, in order to secure a good form for a frequently recurring word or phrase.

Line 2—(First three words).—Express charges, expressage, express agent.

152. "Super" may generally be contracted to sP.

Line 2—(Last three words).—Supersede, superscription, superinduce.

153. The syllable con or com may sometimes be omitted when it occurs in the middle of a word, and the parts joined, if the outline so formed will not conflict with that of some other word.

Line 3.—Incomprehensible, uncontrollable, unconditional, inconvenient, inconsistent.

154. If a negative prefix requires an N sound to be represented, N or n must be used instead of a vowel sign. (See Par. 135.)

Line 4.—Unattainable, unaccomplished, unrequited, unmolested, unhandy.

155. It is sometimes inconvenient to represent both T or D sounds in the past tense of verbs, where the T hook is followed by the T tick; in such cases, omit the T hook and write only the T tick, leaving one of the sounds unrepresented.

Line 5.—Fitted, voted, folded, vaulted, related, resulted, unfolded.

156. Vowels may be joined to final hooks when a superior form results.

Line 6.—Pity, pretty, beauty, Duffy, guffaw, Guiteau, produce.

157. A curve vowel can never follow a circle, as it might be mistaken for the T hook; but the form of a word may sometimes be materially improved by introducing a straight line vowel in this situation.

LINE 7.—Attenuation, dispensation, causation, luxation, annexation, gasoline.

EXAMPLES.—Condensation, compensation, inspissation, accusation.

158. Use a medial vowel rather than the connecting hook when the former affords an equally facile form, especially when vocalization is necessary to legibility.

LINE 8.—Gum, doom, pike, finny, Zeno, rogue.

EXAMPLES.—Dumb, pica, pug (PeuG), puke, Gaza, pony, bony, fop, fob, Beulah, hazy, Gussie, occupy, Willoughby, spoony.

159. Contractions may be suggestively vocalized when desirable for the sake of legibility. This is generally applied in the case of phrasing, subsequently explained.

LINE 9.—Upon, took, object, come, think, shall, put, can.

160. To avoid an awkward form it is sometimes necessary to disjoin parts of words.

LINE 10—(First three words).—Fusible, Grafton, systematize.

161. When two S sounds occur together, one may sometimes be omitted without endangering legibility.

LINE 10—(Last four forms).—Dissimilar, it is said, just such, as soon as.

162. Legibility is greatly improved by indicating the number of syllables by the number of stems, in many words.

LINE 11.—Piccolo, period, coincide, canary, La Paz, Laura, Lima.

LESSON XXV.

USE OF STENOGRAPHIC MATERIAL.

(Illustrated by the Plate on page 196.)

163. It has been said that a discriminating use of the material heretofore given, contrasting the full stems with contracted modifications—such as circles, hooks, etc., having the same sound—renders it possible in many cases to show where the vowel comes in, thus adding to speed by saving the time necessary to write the vowel. I shall endeavor in this lesson to make this important rule clear to the learner, so that he may intelligently apply it whenever necessary.

164. The S circle at the beginning of a word shows unmistakably that S is the first sound in the word; so that, if an initial vowel precedes an S sound, that sound must be represented by the stem.

LINE 12.—Same, asthma, spy, espy, sack, ask, stay, Estey.

EXAMPLES.—Let the student extemporize five pairs.

NOTE 69.—The stem S, however, at the beginning of a word, does not always indicate that a vowel precedes it, for the law of form frequently requires the stem S to represent an initial S sound, as in "something" (SmTh), "sign" (Sn), "send" (Snt).

165. Any circle written at the end of a word indicates unmistakably that that circle represents the last sound in the word; if a vowel should follow the sound represented by the circle, a stem would have to be substituted for the circle.

LINE 13.—Puss, pussy, days, daisy, pain, pony, tin, tiny.

EXAMPLES.—Let the student extemporize ten pairs.

166. When two S or Z sounds are the only consonants in a word, the form of the word is governed by the presence

or absence of a final vowel. If the word ends in a vowel, let it end in the stem; if it does not end in a vowel, let it end in the circle. (See Lesson XIV.)

LINE 14.—Sis, sissy, sauce, saucy, sues, Susie, seize, says.

167. The use of the str loop shows unmistakably that no vowel intervenes between its elements; if a vowel should occur, a stem must be used for at least one of the elements.

LINE 15.—Strip, stirrup, stride, storied, strife, starve, stroll, sterile.

EXAMPLES.—Let the student extemporize ten pairs.

168. The tr loop, or its equivalent en, shows that no vowel can follow its last R sound, a stem being necessary when a vowel follows the sounds represented by the loop.

LINE 16.—Better, betray, voter, votary, ratter, rotary, factor, factory.

EXAMPLES.—Let the student extemporize five pairs.

169. The R and L hooks indicate, as a general rule, that the hook and stem coalesce, with no vowel between them, the stems or reversed L hook being used when a vowel intervenes.

LINE 17.—Plea, pillow, crew, car, flee, fool, throw, thorough.

EXAMPLES.—Let the student extemporize ten pairs.

(The remainder of this lesson is illustrated by the Plate on page 197.)

170. The stem L at the beginning of a word indicates that a vowel precedes it, and the stem L at the end of a word indicates that a vowel follows it. The reversed L hook is used for initial and final L. Any deviations from this rule will be specially noted.

LINE 1.—Elk, luck, Alp, lap, pulley, pull, Kelly, coal.

171. A final hook shows that the word ends in the sound represented by the hook, with no vowel following, while a stem ending a word will generally show that a vowel follows it.

Line 2.—Puff, puffy, doubt, duty, shot, chateau, rate, ready.

172. The sound of W at the beginning of a word should be represented by the W half circle (using w before L, N, and M); if a vowel precedes the W, then use the stem Way.

Line 3.—Wait, await, wake, awake, one, award.

173. Initial "sl" should be represented by sl, but when preceded by a vowel the stem S must be used.

Line 4.—Sleep, slack, slim, sling, asleep, aslope, aslant.

174. Initial "sl" followed by the sound of T, F, V, S, Z, R, N, or tr, without a vowel following them, should be represented by sL; but followed by the sound of D, this combination should be represented by sl followed by the stem D.

Line 5.—Sleet, slave, sluice, slur, slant, slaughter, sled, slide.

Examples.—Slain, slate, slice, slit, slut, slat, Slade.

175. Flexibility or ease of writing requires that final hooks, circles, or loops on straight stems should be written on the side opposite to any initial modification. All final hooks, circles, or loops, except the S circle, obey this law of form; but simple s must always be turned with Backward Motion when joined to straight stems, initially or finally. This law supersedes every other rule except in the case of the S circle.

Line 6.—Serf, snort, summon, consummation, melt, heart, slaughter, less, lights.

NOTE 70.—When the tr loop is turned with Backward Motion on straight stems, its Stenotype becomes dr.

NOTE 71.—This law of form may be followed almost always in the case of the stem L, since its initial hook (unlike all other initial hooks) may be written on either side. This hook is not read, but is only a mark of distinction from the stem R. (See the words "less" and "lights," in Line 6.)

176. The above rule should also be observed when straight stems, modified initially, follow other stems.

LINE 7.—Desert, absolute, accent, examine, answered, wharf.

EXAMPLES.—Let the student extemporize five illustrations.

NOTE 72.—Final modifications on straight stems have been assigned with special reference to the importance of this principle.

177. Flexibility requires the use of *acute* angles, if available, where angles are at all necessary. To secure this, the six stems with two directions should be struck up or down, regardless of any previous rule. Line 8 shows forms to be avoided, while Line 9 shows the proper forms to be used in such cases.

LINE 8—(Improper forms).—Fig, ferry, rock, car, narrow, hovel.

LINE 9—(Proper forms).—Fig, ferry, rock, car, narrow, hovel.

178. In turning a circle inside of a hook, let the circle be elongated into a loop, when both circle and hook will be easily shown. The circle thus modified cannot conflict with another loop, because no loop is ever turned inside of a hook.

LINE 10.—Stray, pets, doves, reads, loads, ends, moods, heads.

179. Following *R* or *L*, N will be found more convenient and faster than n.

LINE 11.—Iron, Perrin, Strathern, saloon, Silurian, silent, salient.

180. The wave signs W, Y, and Ng, should be begun with Forward or Backward Motion, so as to secure a good joining with other stems.

LINE 12.—Awake, acquire, yoke, ink, anxious, being, losing.

181. When the sound of L follows the S circle at the end of a word, with a vowel between the S and the L, the stem El must be used so as to provide a place for the vowel to be written. (See Par. 170.)

LINE 13.—Excel, codicil.

LESSON XXVI.

PHRASING.

(Illustrated by the Plate on page 197.)

182. Phrasing consists in joining the signs of two or more words in a continuous outline, or simply indicating the sounds of those words by the various principles of contraction. This principle should be used with caution; only the most common words should be phrased, and then only when they are naturally grouped together in speaking. Above all, avoid *straining* after phrase-writing, but make the joinings only when they seem natural and easy, and are suggested without any special effort of the memory. Remember, in case of doubt, it is always proper to write words separately and in their correct positions. Let it be laid down as a principle, that the formation of new phrases when in the act of following a speaker is entirely out of the question, and any such futile idea should be dismissed from the mind at once. No phrases are of any practical value except those which have been thoroughly elaborated and committed to memory in the same way as any other contractions. It may be possible to extemporize some phrases under a slow speaker, but as it cannot be done under a fast

one, it is difficult to see the utility of it at all. If one *must* get along without extemporizing phrases under a fast speaker, he certainly *can* get along without it under a slow one.

The opinions here maintained are confirmed by *fac similes* of the actual notes of reporters of all schools.

183. For phrasing purposes, *a*, *an*, or *and* is represented by the vowels A, *A*, or a, according to convenience of joining. They are not joined initially, but only medially or finally. The syllable "ing" may be indicated by nearness, as in the phrases "giving a," "seeing a," etc.

LINE 14.—Is a, as a, with a, for a, giving a, seeing a, finding a.

EXAMPLES.—Can a, which a, judge a, love a, think a, before a, from a, but a.

184. The word "it" may be represented by the T tick when the full form or the T hook cannot be joined.

LINE 15.—Tried it, told it, wished it, signed it, raised it, found it, called it, recollect it.

EXAMPLES.—Stayed it, studied it, faced it, shunned it, shared it, send it, assessed it, roast it, lost it, lent it, named it, mind it, meant it, missed it.

185. The direction of striking an outline is sometimes changed to facilitate joining or phrasing, if legibility be not impaired thereby.

LINE 16.—Of a, to a, thinking of, nothing, we would, would we, think you, it would.

NOTE 73.—The article A is written slanting only in these two instances, being a special arrangement for the two phrases *of a* and *to a*. *Of* is written horizontal when used in the place of the Ing dot, so as not to conflict with *to;* and *a*, *an*, or *and*, in this situation, is always written with the *A* or a vowel sign, to prevent conflict with *of*.

186. The form of a word is sometimes changed to facilitate joining.

LINE 17.—Some, something, any, anything, can be done, shall be done, may be done.

(The remainder of this lesson is illustrated by the Plate on page 198.)

187. The forms for *with, were, where,* and *would,* may be doubled in size to add *you,* or *your; you,* to add *would* or *were.*

LINE 1.—With you, with your, were you, were your, where you, where your, would you, would your, you would, you were.

188. Usually only the first word of a phrase occupies its proper position, the rest of the phrase following, of course, without regard to the rule of position.

LINE 2—(First two forms).—I think so, they shall.

189. But when the first word of the phrase sign belongs to the First Position, it may be written a little higher or lower without being removed from its own position, so that sometimes the second word may also be written in position.

LINE 2—(Last seven forms).—We have, we see, I say, I wish, I shall, I can, is he.

190. The auxiliary verb *have* may be omitted in some phrases where it must necessarily be supplied, and generally, connecting words, which must necessarily and may readily be supplied, may be omitted in common phrases, the connected words being joined, or written near together.

LINE 3.—Can have done, shall have done, year after year, from time to time, from day to day, hour after hour, hours and hours, Word of God.

191. Between figures *or* may be omitted by writing the second figure or figures a little above and to the right of the first; *and,* by writing the second a little below and to the

right of the first; *to*, by leaving a space if the phrase begins with *from;* in fractions, the line between the numerator and denominator may be omitted, and in dates only the last two figures of the present century need be written.

LINE 4.—7 or 8, 6 and 7, from 12 to 14, ⅜, 16½, 1882.

192. The phrase *of the* may frequently be indicated by nearness.

LINE 5.—End of the lesson, arrival of the steamer, words of the text, business of the session, news of the day, yours of the 16th received.

193. A few common words may be written immediately below the line to indicate a preceding *a*, *an*, or *and*. When *of* is written under the line for this purpose, it must be written horizontally to prevent conflict with *to;* and *a* or *an* in this situation must be represented by e to prevent conflict with *of*. This position will constitute a Fourth Position for stem signs which are vertical or inclined. If the writer chooses to write any horizontal stems in this position, they must be depressed at least half the length of the H stem below the line, so as not to interfere with the Third Position. And if *you* is so written, it must also be depressed in the same way to prevent possible conflict with *will*, especially when enlarged to represent *you would* or *you were*.

LINE 6.— And the, and a-an, and I-should, and on-other-O, and of, and to-know-no, and we-with-where, and would, and will, and all-let, and is-his-as-has, and which, and may, a man.

194. *The* may be very generally omitted and indicated by nearness, and *to* may quite often be indicated by the same expedient. In phrasing, *the* may sometimes be represented by the T tick, but only by striking that tick in the direc-

tion of R, as otherwise it might be mistaken for *a* or *an*.

LINE 7.—By the time, in the matter, in the other, I wish to have, time to come, expect to go, with the exception.

195. *The* may be joined in a few advantageous phrases.

LINE 8.—Of the, to the, but the, should the, from the, on the, with the, is the, the more haste the less speed.

EXAMPLES —Could the, know the, were the, where the, as the, has the, will the.

196. In phrasing on simple stems, the circles, loop, and hooks, add as follows: N circle adds *in, an, and, been, own, than;* and when used for the sound of M, adds *may, him, time, my;* tr loop adds *there, their, they are,* and occasionally *other;* R hook adds *are, our, or;* L hook adds *all, will;* T hook adds *it,* and occasionally *the;* F hook adds *of, have, ever.* (Illustrated by Lines 9 to 15 inclusive.) *Than* may sometimes be joined as shown in the last two forms in Line 10.

LINE 9.—Put in, come in, in an, by an, now and then, here and there, have been, had been.

LINE 10.—Have been there, had been there, their own, larger than, rather than, more than, higher than, sooner than, better than.

LINE 11.—It may be, she may be, for him, see him, to him, long time, for my, at my.

LINE 12.—Over there, out there, if their, that they are, there they are, when they are, each other.

LINE 13.—They are, by our, in our, two or three, at all, they will, in all.

LINE 14.—Upon it, for it, say it, while it, in it, upon the, by the, about the, for the.

LINE 15.—Out of, think of, which have, they have, shall have, do you have, did you ever.

NOTE 74.—It must not be supposed that the circles, hooks, etc., here referred to, are to be used in every conceivable case for the words assigned to them. On the contrary, each modification is employed for only a limited number of phrases, where its use is specially advantageous. Their employment beyond the phrase-signs quoted here should be with caution, and where no impairment of legibility will be occasioned. In phrasing, the N or M circle should be turned with Forward Motion on straight stems or ticks, to prevent conflict with the S circle, as in the phrases "in his," "in my" (Nm[f]).

197. Special contractions or phrase signs may be formed by the reporter when needed, always retaining the principal, or at least the initial sounds of the words and phrases so represented.

LINE 16.—Pacific coast, Pacific Mail Steamship Co., Central Pacific Railroad Co., Southern Pacific Railroad Co., Atchison, Topeka and Santa Fe R. R. Co., House of Representatives.

198. Since the nominative and objective cases of pronouns may be represented by the same form without confusion, as in the case of *he* and *him*, so those two words may be indicated by the same circle, *he* being arbitrarily represented in this case for the sake of the very advantageous forms resulting with this frequent word.

LINE 17—(First two forms).—Did he, that he was.

199. *I* may be omitted in such phrases as are shown here, and the L hook may stand for W.

LINE 17—(Last six forms).—That I have, when I am, it was, which was, that was, she was.

200. The phrases *is his, as has*, etc., which would naturally be represented by two separate circles, may be indicated by writing a loop, standing alone and slanting up to the right, for the two circles. *Con* and *com* may be indicated by nearness between words, as well as between syllables. (See Par. 120.) The phrase *to the* may be omitted in certain common phrases, and indicated by nearness, as in *come*

to the conclusion (K-Klshn), *call attention to the fact* (K*l* Tshn-F), where the words *to the* are necessarily supplied. The word *of* may often be omitted, but without writing the words near together. *Been* may sometimes be represented by N, when advantageous in phrases, as in *has not been* (sNtN), *they have been* (DhfN). *Not* may sometimes be represented by N, as in *would not* (*w*[l]N). In a few special phrases *him* may be represented by a horizontal tick, as in *with him* (*w*[l]A); *said*, by the S circle and T hook, as in *he said* (Hst); *not*, by the word sign for *no*, struck vertically when more convenient, as in *we would not* (*wwo*); *let us not* ("let" s "no"); and *year*, by Y, as in *this year* (DhsY).

201. CAUTION.—*We* must not be phrased following other words, nor between words, except where it cannot be mistaken for *you*.

202. Phrasing should be avoided when a pause occurs between the words, or when they do not belong to the same part of the sentence; when the joining would produce an awkward or illegible form; when the phrase would be inconveniently long, or would interfere with the writing on the line above or below.

203. It will be found that phrasing will seldom prove advantageous in phrases of more than two words, and those very frequently recurring. Phrases or contractions that occur so infrequently as to require an effort of the memory to recall them, are a detriment rather than a help to speed, as the hesitation of a moment suffices to write the words separately.

204. The power of using phrases to advantage depends largely on the memory, and the practice should be adopted gradually, as the student finds them necessary. Different

persons will vary in this particular. Many excellent reporters scarcely ever phrase at all, even the most frequent words, and their testimony shows that the faster they write, the less they phrase. These facts only emphasize the remarks at the beginning of this lesson, and show that phrasing is *not* the desideratum which shorthand authors have been wont to pronounce it.

LESSON XXVII.

LIST OF WORD-SIGNS.—PUNCTUATION.

205. Observation shows that fully one-half of ordinary extemporaneous speaking is made up of the repetition of about one hundred common words. A large degree of brevity will obviously be attained by providing brief signs for these frequently recurring words. Many of these do not require further abbreviation than merely omitting the vowels; others contain several consonants, which, if written in full, would be too slow for reporting purposes. These words are represented by signs of adequate brevity, generally requiring but one motion of the pencil, as shown in the following

TABLE OF WORD-SIGNS.

{ Upon
{ Put
{ Part-y

{ Wish
{ Shall
{ Pleasure

{ About
{ What
{ Between

{ Usual-ly
{ Was
{ Recollect

TABLE OF WORD-SIGNS—Continued.

It / Take / Took	Before / There / Regard
At / Out-too / Did	Little / Never / Now
Differ-ence-ent / Dollar-s / Defendant	Knew-new / Than / Time
Do / Which / Change	Make / Matter / Long
Much / Charge / Object	Along / Among / Young
Judge / Large / Advautage	Language / Water / Aware
Common / Kingdom / Come	Your-you are-you / Him / Who-m
Court / Can / Give-n	Have / The / A
God / Together / Go	An / And / Ah
Good / Life / For	Of / To / No
After / Fact / Ever	Know / Oh-owe / Other
Live / Every / Very	Year / Yet / Yon-your
Love / Think / Thing	I / From / But
Worth / Thousand / Thank	Should / Could / Another
Worthy / That / Thou	On / World / Oil-y

TABLE OF WORD-SIGNS—CONCLUDED.

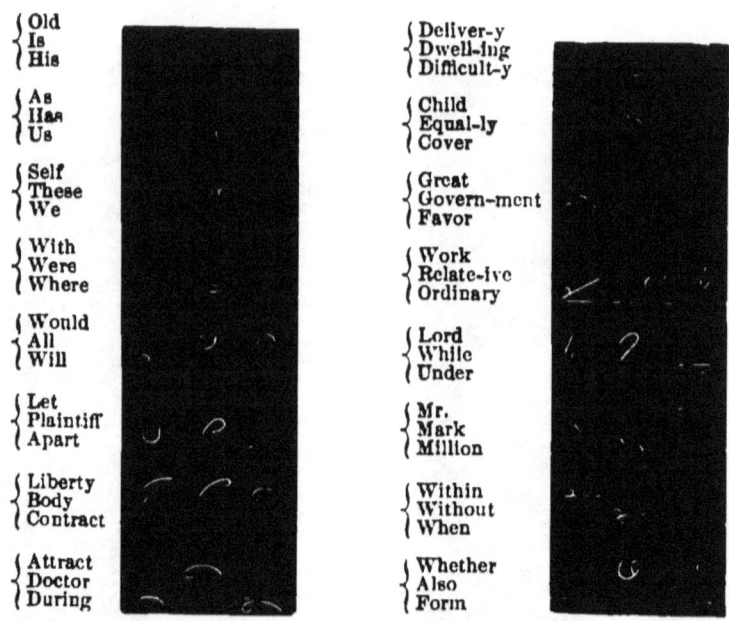

{ Old
{ Is
{ His

{ As
{ Has
{ Us

{ Self
{ These
{ We

{ With
{ Were
{ Where

{ Would
{ All
{ Will

{ Let
{ Plaintiff
{ Apart

{ Liberty
{ Body
{ Contract

{ Attract
{ Doctor
{ During

{ Deliver-y
{ Dwell-ing
{ Difficult-y

{ Child
{ Equal-ly
{ Cover

{ Great
{ Govern-ment
{ Favor

{ Work
{ Relate-ive
{ Ordinary

{ Lord
{ While
{ Under

{ Mr.
{ Mark
{ Million

{ Within
{ Without
{ When

{ Whether
{ Also
{ Form

NOTE 75.—It will be seen that the vowel-signs are made to do duty as word-signs as far as practicable. Many of the ticks or short dash signs may appear arbitrary; they may, however, be considered as vowel-signs varied in direction, or, in some cases, as adapted from the T tick. The small half-circle *w*, and the reversed L hook, used independently, are also utilized. *Year*, *yet*, and *you* are modifications of the u vowel, which sometimes contains the sound of Y. *These* is formed by adding the S circle to the word-sign for *the*. The S circle may be added to word-signs, as to other forms, to form the plural, etc.

NOTE 76.—The least irksome, and perhaps the most expeditious way to commit these word-signs to memory, will be to familiarize them in connection with the exercises which follow.

206. PUNCTUATION, ETC.—For a period, write a small cross on the line, or a long downward R; for an interrogation point, write a small cross above the line, or a long M; for a semicolon, colon, and exclamation point, use the ordinary signs, except that the dots should be represented by small crosses; for a dash, write two long, slanting strokes, joined at the bottom; for a hyphen, write two small,

parallel, horizontal dashes; for quotation marks, leave a space at the beginning of the quotation, and write two small, parallel dashes, slanting up to the right, at the end, as shown in the following table:

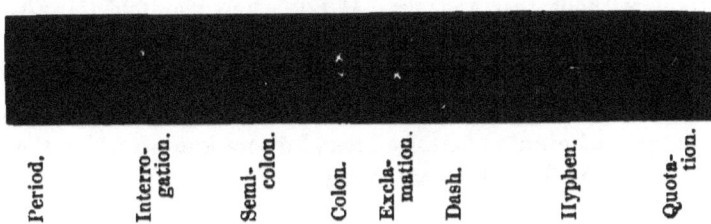

| Period. | Interrogation. | Semi-colon. | Colon. | Exclamation. | Dash. | Hyphen. | Quotation. |

Note 77.—In reporting, spaces may be used for punctuation—half an inch or more for a period, and proportionately less for minor pauses. It is very essential to the correct reading of notes that *dashes* should always be inserted, as the reader should know unmistakably where a break in the sense occurs.

EXAMPLES—(*Introducing word-signs*).—The party were given but two hours in which to get ready. What is the difference between us? Whom would you take with you on this occasion? All whom I know will go with me. Let me row on the bay. May I go down to the city? Of course you may, but put some money in your purse before you say good-bye. The defendant will object to the charge of the judge. I am happy to know that you will dine with us. The company has decided not to issue the summons. It will take many a day to pay the charge. I regard them all as very worthy men. I judge it is worth, anyhow, a thousand dollars. Let us go to the city and buy some toys. What shall we buy for Johnnie? I guess we will get (GT) him a wooden pony (PoN*i*). What would you give for that ranch? I shall take pains to see that they have a good time. It will give me much pleasure to do so. Have you any proof that the receipt was signed? Do you believe that the house belongs to him? The advantages in favor of the relative candidates are about equal. The work was performed under the personal supervision of the author. In our little world the school-master was a great personage. The government was assailed by traitors from within and foes from without. During the delivery of the sermon, much difficulty was met with from the noise without. The expense attending that work will be very great; a million dollars will fall under the mark. The two fierce animals were about equally matched and were writhing in a mortal struggle. Liberty without license should be vouchsafed by every government. The plaintiff claims that the defendant would not give up the child. Mr. Blank is a man who endeavors, I think, to do right, without fear or favor. O Lord, how manifold (MnFlt) are thy works. Charity covers a multitude of sins. When the body was raised, it had begun to decay rapidly (RPt). Doctor, do you think there is any danger that my friend will contract the disease? While I have great admiration for the actress, I do not know whether she will attract the pleasure-seekers of the city.

OMISSION OF VOWELS.

207. At this stage of his practice the writer may begin to omit many unimportant vowels. This should be done gradually, and only so far as words have become familiar to the eye from their consonant outlines alone. To avoid illegibility from too sudden a transition, and until this familiarity extends to all ordinary words, vowels should be omitted only in the following cases:

1st. When the existence of the vowel is shown by the variation of the outline, especially in connection with the two directions for writing R, and the representation of other sounds by stems, or hooks and circles, as in *rose* (Rs), *rosy* (RZ), *herb* (*R*B), *rib* (R*B*), *knave* (Nv), *navy* (N*V*).

2d. Unaccented vowels in words of more than one stem, as in *decay* (DKA), *despise* (DsPs), *enemy* (NM:e).

3d. In words of three or more stems, all medial vowels.

208. On the contrary the writer should retain:

1st. Most accented vowels, except when their place is shown, as *occasion* (Kshn:A).

2d. A diphthong, as in *idea* (*I*D), *decry* (DKr*I*), *toy* (T:awi).

3d. An initial or final vowel, unless indicated by the form of the outline, as in eat (*E*T), gray (Gr*A*).

LESSON XXVIII.

APPLICATION OF SOME OF THE FOREGOING PRINCIPLES. GENERAL DIRECTIONS.

209. Let the pupil write the following examples for practice:

EXAMPLES—(*Words of three stems*).—Pebbly, peacock, package, pigmy, pagoda, apothegm (PThM), punish, becalm, bookish, backache, bugaboo, bigamy, Bogota, baggage, faggot (*F*GT), foppish (FPSh), famish, fathom, farm, evict, vacate, vivify (VV*F*), unpack, nabob, infamy, invoke, Nineveh, inanity, magpie, embalm, mammoth (MMcTh), mimic, mutiny, Madonna, amenity, magic (McJK), hackney, hoggish.

(*Words of four stems*).—Tippecanoe, toothpick, decoct, pitch-pipe, Piccadilly, Poughkeepsie.

(*Words of two stems, the first with initial circle*.)—Speech, speak, spear, spare, sapper, Spohr, supper, spire, set-to, stony, Sidney, Sodom, skip, scoop, scab, scabby, sketch, Scotch, scathe (sKcDh), scare, scar, score, scour, skinny, Sachem, notched, knocked.

(*Words of two stems, with N circle between*).—Pinch, Pancho, punch, paunch, pansy (*P*). Panama, bench, banjo, bunch, beneath, banish, banner, Benham, tinge, tinner, tanner, dainty, dandy, Dingie, dinner, jaunty, Jenner, county, candy, gunner, affinity, finite, Finch, finish, fancy, finer, vanity, vanish, venom.

(*Words of two stems, the first with a final hook*).—Petite, potato, potash (*P*), Patsey (*P*), epitome, buttock, beatify (*F*), beautify (*F*), Betsey (*B*), battery, button, bidden, batten, bottom, buffet, toughen, tighten, deaden, shaven, soften, rotary, written, retain, rotten, river, reverie, rover, lottery, lighten.

GENERAL DIRECTIONS.

210. The diligent student of the preceding pages has now become tolerably familiar with a large proportion of the words used in ordinary public speaking. The application of the system to the principal branches of verbatim reporting will be shown in the copious exercises in reporting which are contained in succeeding pages. Paper for reporting should be ruled with lines about half an inch apart, with but little gloss on the surface, so as to be plainly written on with a pencil of medium quality, that being the implement generally used by practical reporters. Pencil writing in this system is as legible as pen writing, there being no shading required. The size of characters should be, as nearly as practicable, the same as those given in the exercises in this book, though in actual practice the tendency will be to make them larger. This inclination should not be humored to the extent of allowing the writing to become sprawling and carelessly executed, for this will be a detriment to speed by giving the hand too long a road to travel. Some careful writers may, and will, write a smaller hand than that in the exercises.

After the writer has become quite familiar with ordinary connected writing, and can write with some freedom from his own reading, he should commence writing from dictation by a reader, selecting from matter which has been spoken off-hand rather than that which has been elaborately composed, since the writer is seldom or never called upon to report the latter. The reader should proceed fast enough to tax the powers of the writer, though not to the extent of confusing him. Part of the time for practice should be devoted to reading back what is written, observing carefully any errors that may be made in deciphering the notes. Each writer should study his own peculiarities of execution, and observe where he is liable to deviate too greatly from the proper outlines. It is of the *utmost importance* to read everything that is written.

To attain the highest speed the writer should go back to the elementary principles, practicing from the alphabet itself, following through all the principles of contraction, writing from dictation, until no hesitation is experienced. It is not necessary to *try* to write rapidly. Thorough familiarity with shorthand outlines and principles is the essential of speed.

In reporting, the commencement of a sentence or phrase should be written with special care, as the context is a necessary aid to reading reporting notes, and if the first part of a sentence is unmistakable, the facility of reading the rest will be greatly enhanced.

The legibility of any rapid system of shorthand is only suggestive, although this suggestiveness is unerring, provided proper attention is paid to the context. The importance of keeping the mind on the *qui vive* in taking notes, to catch the varying forms of expression and the sequence of ideas, cannot be over-estimated, as such attention is indispensable to the getting out of a first-class transcript. The reporter must use his own judgment as to the liability of words conflicting in any particular case, and if in doubt, should drop in a vowel so as to be on the safe side. Proper nouns and infrequent words should be made unmistakable by the insertion, when necessary, of at least one prominent vowel.

Interruptions from the audience in the course of a speech

may be noted in shorthand, and large circles drawn around them, or inclosed in a parenthesis if more extended; and as time is generally limited, only the last curve of the parenthesis need be written, leaving a space at the beginning of the interruption. This practice may be followed whenever a parenthesis is introduced for any purpose. Should the reporter from any cause fail to catch a word or words of the speaker, a large circle may be written in the place of the omission, and a space corresponding to the words omitted may be left. A line down the margin of the page calls attention to something in the passage opposite. In reporting meetings where speakers are unknown, they may be numbered 1, 2, 3, etc., and their names learned afterward.

The repetition of a phrase by the speaker may be indicated by drawing a long horizontal line in the place of the repeated words after they have been once written.

In quotations from the Bible or other book, the book, chapter, and verse, or similar divisions, may be designated by writing them in the First, Second, and Third Positions respectively.

In idiomatic expressions, such as "deeper and deeper," "stronger and stronger," "quicker and quicker," the first word may be contracted to good advantage without endangering legibility, and the connecting words omitted, as in deeper and deeper (DDPR), stronger and stronger (strNg-strNgR), etc.

In his early practice, after attaining a speed of about 120 words a minute from dictation, the writer should commence writing after some careful, deliberate speaker, taking care to write only what can be deciphered afterward. He should not be led into the error of dashing along recklessly, and making marks that can never reproduce the words for which they stand. When the writer knows he is taking legible notes, the confidence imparted adds to his speed. Vowels should be inserted quite frequently at first, wherever any doubt arises as to legibility. Practice alone will enable the reporter to determine the extent to which vocalization is necessary, since different temperaments will require different degrees of suggestiveness in outline. A person with a poor memory will require a fuller style than one who rarely forgets anything pictured to the eye. Good spellers in the ordinary print will be found to be good readers of shorthand.

Let the young reporter not be impatient at his early failures in the acquirement of speed and the ability to read his rapid notes, but remember he is traveling the same road that every good reporter must travel, and that in this, as in other departments of life, "there is no royal road to knowledge." Nothing is of much value which does not require much labor to attain it.

REPORTING EXERCISES.

The teacher must use his judgment as to the amount of matter to be assigned for a lesson in the following exercises. Perhaps a page of the notes will be sufficient at first, the amount being extended as the pupil acquires a knowledge of connected writing. The following exercises illustrate the five branches of Business, Law, Political, Lecture, and Sermon reporting. Thorough acquaintance with them, both in writing and reading, will contribute largely to the efficiency of the student. Armed with a knowledge of shorthand which these exercises afford, he will essay the reporting of ordinary speakers with good assurances of success.

It will, of course, be understood that the selections here

given do not embody the opinions of the author in reference to the subjects treated therein. They have been chosen with a view to furnishing the most valuable exercises for the student, embracing various subjects and a wide range of terms. Thorough familiarity with them, both in reading and writing, will be the student's best preparation for actual work, as thereby he will become possessed of a knowledge of all the most common words and phrases that enter into ordinary extemporaneous speaking. They should first be read until the forms have become familiar to the eye, and then written repeatedly from dictation until a speed has been attained of upward of a hundred words a minute for five minutes at a time. Then every opportunity should be embraced to report public speakers, and this should be commenced as soon as possible, for the confidence in one's powers which is imparted from knowing that he *can* do something, is very essential to his further advancement in the art.

BUSINESS REPORTING.

KEY TO NOTES COMMENCING ON PAGE 199.

Fireman's Fund Insurance Company,
San Francisco, July 25, 1882.

Mr. Richard Roe, Agt., Ashland, Ogn.

Dear Sir :—Your telegram of even date announcing loss under our policy No. 80965 is at hand, and we have advised you by telegraph to see that the assured properly protects his goods from further damage, awaiting the arrival of our adjuster. Our Special Agent Ives, who is now in Portland, has been telegraphed to, and in a few days will be with you. In the meantime it might expedite matters if you would have the assured classify and arrange such property as has been saved, making a list thereof, so that when our adjuster arrives matters may be settled in the least possible time. We always desire to settle up a loss as speedily as possible, and hope that you will coöperate with us to this end. Please do not commit the company on any points which may arise, but confine yourself exclusively to the matters suggested.

Referring to your favor of the 22d inst., just at hand, with reference to the proposed cancellation of Mr. Smith's policy, we have to say that you are correct in your supposition that it will be necessary to charge him short rates for the time policy has been in force. This for 4 mos. will be five-tenths the annual rate, and you will therefore pay him back one-half his premium, taking his receipt therefor on the policy, and returning latter to us. If, however, Mr. Smith is merely desirous of removing to a new location, we would suggest that we would be willing to make a transfer of the policy, by endorsement thereon, charging additional rate pro rata for the increased hazard in the new location.

We enclose herewith our policy No. ———, as applied for. The rate as named by you in the application is technically correct, but where an exposure over ten feet distant consists of a long frame range we charge more than the regular tariff rate. The charge for exposure as provided in the book of rates is just the same whether the risk which is ten feet or more away consists of a single building or of a frame range of a dozen buildings. The hazard in the latter case is manifestly much greater than in the former, but it would be impossible to fix a tariff which would apply to all cases; so the only thing left for the companies is to exercise their judgment in such cases. You must not make the mistake of supposing that the rates named in the rate-book are those which are fixed definitely for all risks, but they are the rates below which no company is allowed to write, and it is the privilege and duty of companies to make their figures as much higher than those in the rate-book as circumstances seem to demand.

Yours truly, E. W. CARPENTER, Ass't Sec'y.

CENTRAL PACIFIC RAILROAD,
OAKLAND, Cal., July 28, 1882.

J. E. WALMSLEY, ESQ., Agt., Washington.

Dear Sir:—I hand you herewith letter from Mr. Fillmore, enclosing complaint from Ehrman & Lebrecht, of Mission San Jose, about delays of freight,

I wish you would go thoroughly into this matter and find out just what freight it is they refer to, the car in which it was received, the way-bill number, and all particulars. Also give me any information that you can which would be of assistance, and return the papers with your reply. Yours truly,

A. D. WILDER, D. S.

CASHIER'S OFFICE A. L. BANCROFT & CO.,
721 MARKET ST., SAN FRANCISCO, June 19th, 1882.

S. H. PAYNE, ESQ., 9 Burling Slip, New York.

Dear Sir:—We have the news of the disaster of ship "Charger." As she has returned to New York with cargo badly damaged by fire and water, we would like to have our goods taken out, and if in good condition, re-shipped to us by railroad, and those goods which might be badly damaged retained in New York to be sold at auction or disposed of otherwise,—*i. e.*, we do not wish to incur any additional expense on damaged stock. We authorize you herewith to act in our name and take such measures as may be necessary to secure possession of our goods, and therefore inclose our original bills of lading, together with a memorandum showing the eastern cost of said shipments. You may, if it is required, pay the clipper freight, make a deposit, or give bond on account of general average, and make such reasonable concessions as will facilitate matters generally. It is of great importance that we should know the extent of the damage as soon as possible, that we may be able to duplicate some of our orders if necessary. We cannot permit our goods to be re-shipped by another clipper, as they would reach us too late for our fall trade. By giving your prompt attention to these important matters you will greatly oblige Yours truly,

A. L. BANCROFT & CO.,
C. BACHMAN.

OFFICE OF FEIGENBAUM & CO., IMPORTERS,
SAN FRANCISCO, Sept. 6th, 1882.

MR. A. LIPMAN, Francfort-on-the-Main.

Dear Sir:—You will please ship by first Sailing Vessel leaving Hamburg—

3275/1   36 dozen Palmleaf Baskets.
2006   24   "   China Tea Sets.
         24   "   Muslin Dolls, each $ 2, 4, 6, 8.
3417   36   "   Bohemian Blue Glass Vases.
4916   12   "   Violins in Boxes with Bow.
3116/2   18   "   Noah's Arks.

We need these goods badly. You therefore will hurry up shipment of same, and oblige   Yours truly,
                                       FEIGENBAUM & CO.

OFFICE OF SHERMAN, CLAY & CO.,
SAN FRANCISCO, Sept. 7, 1882.

MESSRS. J. ESTEY & CO., Brattleboro, Vt.

Gentlemen:—Please send us by sail through our agent M. R. Cusack, 61 South St., New York, 5 style 1, 10 style 2, 20 style 521, 25 style 280, 25 style 281, 10 style 330, 5 style 96. At your request we remind you to prepay the freight to New York.

Yours respectfully,   SHERMAN, CLAY & Co.

MR. A. WEBER, 5th Ave., cor. 16th St., N. Y.

Dear Sir:—Please forward by sail as heretofore, through our agent M. R. Cusack, 61 South St., 20 style 1 uprights, 10 style 2 uprights, 15 style 3 uprights, 10 style 1 squares, 5 parlor grands, and 2 concert grands. Please be particular to observe our instructions to place a thin piece of wood back of the silk panels in the uprights. Carefully observe this in all shipments of uprights by sail, and oblige

Yours truly,
                                       SHERMAN, CLAY & CO.

MRS. JOHN DOE, Nevada City.

Dear Madam:—In reply to yours of the 6th instant inquiring prices of instruments, etc., we mail you to-day catalogues of the Weber Piano, and of the Estey and Sterling Organs. Our regular selling price for the Weber is $100 less than the printed prices in the catalogue, making style 1 upright or square cost you $550. We will include good stool and cover with each instrument. If you wish to purchase on the installment plan, we will accept $100 cash, and $25 or more per month, with interest on the deferred payments at the rate of one per cent. per month.

From the Estey catalogue we will give you a discount of — per cent., and from the Sterling catalogue — per cent. on any style you may select. As you are a teacher, we shall be pleased to allow you the regular professional discount on sheet music, namely — off from retail price.

Trusting that we may be favored with your patronage, we remain
      Yours respectfully,
         SHERMAN, CLAY & CO.

Mr. John Smith, Seattle, W. T.

Dear Sir:—Replying to your favor of the 31st ultimo, we mail you to-day our catalogue of musical merchandise, on page 55 of which you will find full descriptions and prices of brass instruments. As we carry only first-class goods in stock, we are confident you will do well to favor us with an order. Awaiting your reply, we are
      Yours truly,
         SHERMAN, CLAY & CO.

LAW REPORTING.

Notes in Law Reporting are usually taken on paper having a marginal line near the left side of the page, and in taking testimony, the questions by counsel, the court, or others, extend to the left of the line, while the answers of witnesses are confined to some distance to the right of the line. This is called Indenting, and serves to distinguish the questions and answers, and facilitates reference to any part of the notes when the reporter is called on to read particular portions of the testimony. An answer following a question on the same line may be separated from it by twice the usual space left for a period, or by the interrogation point; and a question following an answer on the same line may be separated from it by the long period. If the writer chooses to write solid instead of indenting, he may do so by placing the long interrogation point at the end of each question, and the long period at the end of each answer. Any extended directions as to the methods of procedure in courts of justice will be inadequate to render the reporter fit for that work, and the only practical way is to familiarize himself with the practice of any court he may expect to enter as a stenographer, by actual observation. This is the necessary method pursued by all reporters of limited experience, and should be adopted by all beginners.

A law reporter should have some knowledge of law, and should be familiar with the rules of evidence, before he will be competent to perform the duties of a court reporter. The taking of testimony is generally the simplest form of reporting which a shorthand writer is called on to do, but the reporting of the pleas of counsel will sometimes tax his powers to the utmost, as in this he is liable to be plied with words from a rich vocabulary.

In the following extracts from the celebrated Schroder trial I shall endeavor to give a general outline of the manner of preparing a report. In the transcript of the notes, questions and answers should be designated by the letters Q. and A., written just to the left of the marginal line found on legal cap paper. Any references to the Court, counsel, or witnesses, should also be commenced to the left of the line.

In taking the notes in shorthand, the name of a witness

should be written in longhand when he is called, to insure proper spelling of it. Cross examinations and other headings in the notes may be made conspicuous by leaving a blank line and writing the headings in shorthand.

KEY TO NOTES COMMENCING ON PAGE 205.

SUPERIOR COURT, NO. 2.

THE PEOPLE
vs.
EDWARD F. SCHRODER.
} BEFORE JUDGE GREEN AND A JURY.

OAKLAND, Dec. 2, 1880.

APPEARANCES.

For *Plaintiff*, Dist. Att'y GIBSON and ZACH. MONTGOMERY.
For *Defendant*, W. W. FOOTE, A. A. MOORE, and HALL MCALLISTER.

The above case coming on for trial, the Court ordered the Official Reporter, —— ——, to take down in shorthand the testimony and proceedings.

Ass't Dist. Att'y WELLS WHITEMORE opens for the prosecution:

The information which was read yesterday charged this client, Edward F. Schroder, with murder on the 26th day of July of the present year, in killing by shooting, of Dr. Alfred Le Fevre. The alleged place of the occurrence was on the northwest corner of 8th Street and Broadway, as shown by the diagram. (Counsel read from the codes, defining murder.) The facts in this case which the prosecution expect to show are, that Dr. Le Fevre, on the afternoon of this shooting, while engaged at his practice as a dentist, was filling a lady's tooth, when this defendant entered one of the rooms shown on the diagram, and a pistol-shot was heard. Immediately after, Dr. Le Fevre came staggering into the next room and died shortly afterwards. This defendant walked into the hall, and was there met by an officer. He gave up the pistol he held in his hand, saying, "Officer, do your duty;

I have shot a man; he seduced my wife. No man can seduce my wife and live." On the way to the city prison he used much the same language. We expect to prove this fact and some others. * * * *

HORATIO STEBBINS sworn for the Defense.

Examined by Mr. MCALLISTER.

Q. Where do you reside?
A. In San Francisco.

Q. How long have you resided in California?
A. Sixteen years.

Q. You are the father of Mrs. Schroder, I believe, Dr. Stebbins?
A. I am.

Q. When did Mr. and Mrs. Schroder take up their residence in Oakland? Do you recollect? About how long ago?
A. Four years ago the 1st of October.

Q. In June, 1880—on the 11th of June—how many children did they have alive at that time?
A. Two.

Q. About what were the ages of these children?
A. One is five; the other is three and a half, or four.

Q. What was the oldest child, a boy or a girl?
A. A boy.

Q. And the younger is a girl?
A. The younger is a girl. * * * * *

Q. What was the question Mr. Schroder asked him?
A. Were you at 1164 Alice St. last night?

Q. What did he reply?
A. After hesitating he answered No.

Q. Anything else said by Schroder?
A. "You were," and he gave him some title of rascal, or scoundrel, something of that kind.

Q. Then you left?
A. He told him also substantially what I had told him—never to look upon him or his wife.

Q. During this interview what was the appearance or manner of Le Fevre?

A. His manner was cowed and abject. He didn't look me in the face.

Q. You were not armed at that time, were you, Mr. Stebbins?

A. No, sir.

Q. Was Schroder armed, to your knowledge?

A. No, sir.

Q. You said you struck him; do you mean you struck him with your hand in the scuffle, or with your fist; how was that?

A. I struck him with my fist.

Q. On the shoulder, sir?

A. Yes, sir.

Q. It was not an attempt to strike him down, but an attempt to draw his attention?

A. If that was his shoulder, I struck him like that. (A loud slap that could be heard over the court-room.)

Q. Did you ever see Dr. Le Fevre after that interview?

A. No, sir.

Q. This was on the 12th of June, as I understand it?

A. The 12th of June.

Q. After that, where did Mr. Schroder and yourself go?

A. We went back on Alice Street.

Dr. J. J. KENDRICK sworn for the Defense.

Examined by Mr. MCALLISTER.

Q. Where do you reside, and what is your business?

A. I am a physician and surgeon, residing in Oakland. Have resided here over two years.

Q. Are you familiar with the general doctrine of insanity as given in the books?

A. I am somewhat.

Q. Have you had occasion to look into the matter?

A. Yes.

Q. Can you give Dr. Bucknell's definition of insanity?

A. The definition of Dr. Bucknell is "a state of mind in which a wrong act of conception or judgment has been committed where violent excitement, or undue circumstances of an exciting nature have been separately or conjointly the cause of disease, either mental or physical"—in fact, what is known as disease of any kind affecting the body or mind in their action. I know the work by Ray. Have read it. It is an authority. Insanity is a disease, sometimes temporary, sometimes permanent. Mania signifies a general derangement of the intellectual faculties, with an easy excitement of the emotions at trifling causes. Monomania is somewhat similar, but the derangement is in reference to but one subject. Dementia refers rather more to the power of the mind—a man cannot command his ideas.

Q. Is dementia more like idiocy than either mania or monomania?

A. Yes, it is more so. It is the idiocy of a fully developed mind.

Q. What is impulsive or transitory insanity?

A. It is the actual emotion of the feelings.

Q. May an insane act be committed with design and deliberation?

(Objected to by the Prosecution. Sustained.)

Q. Do you know what an insane impulse is?

A. It is hard to define. It is rather a notorious fact that the insane exhibit and betray a wonderful cunning. In the words of a text-book, "A crime is often committed so cunningly that the act itself is the only evidence of insanity."

SARAH J. GALLAGER recalled.

Cross-examined by Mr. MONTGOMERY.

Mr. MONTGOMERY. We wish to ask this witness a few questions by way of cross examination, on points we didn't think of at the time at which she was here.

Q. You testified yesterday that you lived at a convent at Sacramento?
A. Yes.
Q. What convent?
A. St. Joseph's.
Q. How long were you there?
A. Nine months.
Q. What were you doing there?
A. I was a laundress there.
Q. When was that?
A. Before I came to Mr. Schroder's.
Q. Immediately before?
A. I had just come from the convent, and came right down to Mr. Schroder's.
Q. Was it immediately before you came to Mr. Schroder's?
A. No, sir; it was three months that I had chills and fever, and had to get into the country for my health, and I left there and came right down to Schroder's.
Q. How long did you live at Sacramento?
A. I cannot tell you.
Q. About how many years?
A. I didn't live there many years. I think I lived about thirteen months at Sacramento—that is, between the convent and Mr. Nash's, at Nicolaus, Sutter County.
Q. I understand that you were at some convent in San Francisco?
A. When was that? I went to the other convent—the Sisters of Charity.
Q. Whereabouts?
A. They are in South San Francisco.
Q. There are several establishments there; where did you live?
A. I lived in the new house where the children were, in the other one.
Q. At the Magdalen Asylum, was it?
A. No, sir; it is not at the Magdalen Asylum.

CLOSE OF THE CHARGE.

And now to conclude, gentlemen. If you shall believe from the evidence before you, beyond, and to the exclusion of all reasonable doubt, that the defendant, Edward F. Schroder, on the 26th day of July, 1880, at and in the county of Alameda and the State of California, did willfully, unlawfully, feloniously, and with malice aforethought, shoot, kill, and murder one Alfred Le Fevre, the person mentioned in the information, then he is guilty of murder in the first degree, and that should be your verdict; and in case you shall find a verdict of that character, it is at your discretion to say, and you should say in your verdict, whether the defendant shall suffer death, or imprisonment in the State Prison for life. Failing to find a verdict of murder in the first degree, you will acquit the defendant. And further, if you shall believe from the evidence, that the defendant did, at the time and place alleged in the information, shoot and kill Alfred Le Fevre, the person mentioned in the information, and if you further believe that the evidence in the case shows that the insanity of the defendant at the time of the killing, has been established by preponderance of proof before you, and that such insanity was such as has been already defined as rendering a person irresponsible for his acts, then the defendant is entitled to an acquittal, and such should be your verdict. And if you shall, upon consideration of all the evidence before you, entertain a doubt whether such insanity of defendant at the time of the killing has been established by preponderance of proof, then you will give the defendant the benefit of the doubt and acquit him.

POLITICAL REPORTING.

KEY TO NOTES COMMENCING ON PAGE 212.

Extracts from the Speech of the Hon. Emory A. Storrs, at Germania Hall, Oakland, September 17, 1880.

(Reported by the Author.)

Mr. Chairman and Fellow Citizens:—I am satisfied that this is a Nation. [Applause.] I am satisfied that the men and women of this beautiful city by the Pacific Sea, have had something to do with making it a nation. I am satisfied that the people of this coast, which I have the honor and pleasure of visiting for the first time, are determined that it shall continue to be a Nation. I am satisfied that they are resolutely resolved that no Solid South and no Democratic party shall endanger its existence as a nation. I am satisfied that they are resolved that the Democratic party, North and South, solid or otherwise, shall be pulverized finer than powder next November, before they are permitted to interfere with the prosperity of this nation.

I am satisfied that that old nerve and muscle, that loftiness of spirit, that heartiness of patriotic purpose, that devotion to a great cause and the great principle which put hundreds of thousands of our sons into the field during four years of war, will save this nation for all time to come, as the custodian of the priceless treasure of free government among men. [Applause.] I have been about this country much, from the east to the west, and from the north to the south. I have sometimes seen larger audiences than are assembled here to-night; I have never (and I am speaking no words of flattery) seen an audience in which I felt more emphatically the influences of the old Republican spirit, that it is perfectly obvious, pervades, fills, and inspires this audience to-night. [Applause.] We need just such audiences; we need just such men and women; we require not only this year, but for many years to come, just such a spirit as is here and now exhibited. It is quite customary, I am aware, for political speakers to preface their address by observation, to the effect that the immediate canvass of the issues which they are discussing is most important in its character. It is my solid judgment, that never since 1860 have we confronted a campaign where the issues have been of more pressing importance, of more serious gravity, than those which we must decide within two months from this time—less than two months from this time. I have no sort of doubt as to what that decision shall be, none whatever. I have no more doubt that there will be for Garfield and Arthur [applause] a solid North, than that there will be for Hancock and English a solid South. I have no more doubt that the Republican ticket will triumph, than I have doubts of the goodness of God, and I have no doubt about that. Boy and man, I have always believed very much more in the goodness of God, than I have in the nimbleness and dexterity of the devil; therefore I have pinned my faith as a matter of expediency to the Republican party. [A voice, "Hit 'em again, Storrs."] Frequently. [Laughter and applause.] I have no doubt, none whatever, as to the absolutely diabolic character of the Democratic party as a political entity. I have no question that as a political organization its aims are wicked, its purposes dangerous, its policy demagogical, and its entire scope and character unpatriotic. I haven't a particle of doubt about it; I have no sort of doubt that had it succeeded at any time, at any general election since 1860, we should have had no country and no history since that time of which to be proud; and I have no more doubt that the Republican party, since 1856—since the day it had its national birth—has combined within itself all that there has been in our politics, patriotic, lofty, generous, humane, and democratic. * * * * * * I have listened to that distinguished Democrat, James R. Doolittle, talking very eloquently on this subject of conciliation, and I have noticed since I have left home, Mr. Doolittle has made a very eloquent speech, in which he appeals to the story of the Prodigal Son, as illustrating what he conceives to be the proper policy for this Government to pursue toward what he called our erring brethren of the South. I was much impressed with his speech and with the story. But two or three days since, at the Palace Hotel, having ample time and abundant opportunity, I got down the New Testament, which is in my room [laughter], and consulted the Gospel according to St. Luke, read the story as there told, and, as I am disposed to believe the Scripture portion of this discussion, for your entertainment I would like to give you my exegesis of that story as their true present political condition. I thought, Mr. Chairman, that I discovered, after the careful reading of the story of the Prodigal Son, one difference between the case put by Senator Doolittle and the case of our Southern brethren.

In the first place the prodigal son of the Scripture, when he had reached his majority, had a perfect right to leave home. That, I see, is not questioned in the parable. In the next place, I discover that he did not take a dollar that did not belong to him. [Applause.] He simply called for his portion, and it was given to him, and it was his. Now, that poor, absurd, foolish boy had a perfect right to leave home. That it was absurd, that it was foolish in him to do so, we all know; and he soon thereafter discovered.

Our Southern brethren, as I understand it, had no such right; and, unless our memories are entirely at fault with regard to that transaction, when they undertook to leave the old mansion they started off with a good deal of property, real and personal, to which they had no rightful ownership. The Scripture prodigal, bearing with him the blessing of his father and his brother, whom he had left behind, went out into the world as many a foolish boy has done since, anxious to see the world, crude, inexperienced in all his notions—a very good-hearted boy, though, after all; lavish with his money, fell among Democrats, and was, naturally enough [applause], after about two weeks' experience with them, cleaned out. After his money was gone his Democratic friends had no further use for him. He went into the pork trade—he went to feeding swine, and they rejected him; even the Greenbackers of those days wouldn't have anything to do with him, and then he went to feeding with the swine. That arrangement was not satisfactory to the swine, and after a few weeks of that experience the poor boy, without enough left of him to address a letter to his father; his clothes and his credit all gone; worse than any tramp you ever saw; as hungry as a modern Democrat, who has been dieting on the east wind for twenty years, and within the last four days shouting over a victory in Maine that he hasn't got [applause], concluded that playing prodigal didn't pay. Looking the ground all over, he discovered that he could not declare anything on the prodigal business beyond a husk dividend. Thoroughly repentant, it not entering into his mind that he had any right—having no such insolence as that he would go back and be conciliated by his father—started back home, and afoot. He was not attended with a hand-wagon, saying that he had come back to be conciliated, and that he would run Congress and hold the balance of the offices; and that poor old father, which stands for our supposed Union in this trouble, standing at the gate looking down that long and dusty turnpike, knowing that the boy would by-and-by come back, for that his heart would turn with tenderness to his own home, saw him coming and ran out to meet him, and he threw his arms about his neck, and the boy fell on his father's neck, as repentant and sorry and thoroughly converted a prodigal as ever you saw in all the days of your life. Now, what was it that the father gave to the returning prodigal? That is the question. What did he do with him? In the first place I notice that the prodigal did not say, "Father, I have concluded to come back and accept the situation and take charge of the farm. I will turn the boy that has stayed at home here out of its possession." He said nothing of the sort. What did he get? Read to-night, after you go home (if you have time enough after this lecture, which is doubtless going to be very long), read to-night the kind of a proposition that the old man made, and what the old father did. Now he didn't give him a dollar in money. He didn't give him a foot of land. He offered him no position whatsoever. He didn't suggest that the boy might have an office; he didn't even reconstruct him. He gave him a veal dinner. [Laughter.] That was no great shakes. [Increased laughter.] There was no market there for calves. He put a ring upon his finger, and the boy asked to be taken in as a servant; simply sought the privilege to do kitchen work, and that was the position which was assigned to him, and he has been doing it ever since. And even then the loyal stay-at-home son that represents our North, stood there and looked at that boy, with the fuss that was made over him and said to his father: "I have never gone off wasting my substance in riotous living; you have never killed any fatted calf for me; you have never put any ring on my finger." But the old man turns round to the loyal son of the North and says: "Son, thou wert always with me; all that I have is thine. Not a dollar of money, not a foot of ground, not an office nor a smell of an office goes to these Southern Brigadiers; but all that I have is thine." It is the saddest thing in all this world to think of, that in about fifteen years since this war has closed—the most wicked and the most causeless which the world has ever witnessed; in less than fifteen years we find that party which sought the destruction of this great nation ruling in its counsels; we find the Southern Brigadier, who fifteen years ago, with sword drawn and arm lifted would rend this fair fabric to pieces, elevated to power; we find Ben Hill and Pillow, Forrest and Wade Hampton and Chalmers—the whole solid, treasonable, rebellious and defeated South—in less than fifteen years after their defeat, in the councils of the nation; in the councils of the nation they sought to destroy, cutting down the army of the Union which defeated them, and sitting in judgment as to the amount of money that shall be paid to Phil. Sheridan and Tecumseh Sherman.

Now there is no nation on the face of God's green earth that ever permitted a thing of that sort before. * * * * * *
And now, my good friends of this splendid coast, with your short but your glorious career behind you, with the future so splendid that none can pen or picture it, what shall your position be? You are a young people; you are a young State; you cannot stay in this old sepulcher of the Democratic party. It is full of dead men's bones and all uncleanness. Come out into the day; come out into the sunshine. Lift your eyes from the narrow partisanship of the old time, and look out upon the broad ocean of freedom. You cannot begin to tell how much braver and better you will feel when you are inspired by these impulses that take in a whole nation; and we shall, Mr. President, succeed. There is no power that can defeat it. You and I don't care where in this great procession we may stand. We only wait for the music; we only listen for the order to march, and we march. We keep step to the music of the Union, and we know it when we hear it; and we know that, great as this continent is, vast as is the sky which bends above it, there is not air enough in all to float but one flag, and that is the flag under which we stand. I recognize it; I hail and I salute it; and I know, just as sure as the day succeeds the night, that Garfield and Arthur carrying the old standard, all that I can be called upon to do is to face the music, follow the flag, and this grand nation of ours shall stand preëminent on the topmost peaks of historic renown and glorious achievement. Worthy of its past, worthy of its sons, worthy of its history, worthy of its future, I heard the word given, "Forward." Let us all join in the march.

KEY TO NOTES COMMENCING ON PAGE 220.

SPEECH OF DR. J. C. SHORB, AT THE DEMOCRATIC STATE CONVENTION, HELD AT SAN JOSE, CAL., IN JUNE, 1882.

Mr. Chairman and Gentlemen of the Democratic State Convention:—
I rise with heartfelt pleasure, as pure as I have ever experienced in my political life, with unshaken loyalty to the interests and the welfare of the Democratic party, and deep solicitude for its vital necessities, to place in nomination for Governor of the State of California,

Clay Webster Taylor, of Shasta. Mr. Chairman, I love California with all my heart and all my soul. I reached her shores many years ago, when still a boy, and from that time to the present moment she has been a mother to me. I feel for her a love, a kindly interest, a bond of sympathy. She has buried in oblivion all my sins and my transgressions. The little merit she has found in me she has exalted a thousand fold. Were I to tell a man east of the Rocky Mountains, and announce to him my love of California, he would say it was affectation or hypocrisy.

Sometimes I feel assured that when the Lord Almighty created the universe, and looked around and said it was very good, he resolved on a new piece of creation and made California. I wish her from my heart all peace and honor, glory and prosperity. Thus loving California, I want to see her Governor a man whose courage, whose intellect and integrity, give promise of as bright and fortunate a future as the destiny of California itself—a natural-born leader of men, a natural Tribune of the people, and one who will become their idol when, in the course of time, they find that ambition cannot reach, aggregated wealth frighten, or gold soil the fair white hand at the Helm of State. Before the Lord, I believe that I present such a character in the person of Clay Webster Taylor. Why, Mr. Chairman, as I pronounce those names—Clay, Webster, Taylor—what a panorama of history presents itself to my contemplation; of Clay, when the story of valor, chivalry, patriotism, and genius is told in the University of the future, it shall echo and ring with the name and genius of Harry Clay, Kentucky's favorite son. And when history writes the dangers surrounding the infancy of this republic, that threatened the disruption of this empire —this glorious empire—this glorious empire of free and co-equal States, how brilliant in the sombre twilight of the past glows the giant form of Webster, whose matchless words, still ringing in our ears, "liberty and union, now and forever, one and inseparable," are as fresh to us to-day as when they fell like molten lava on the ears of the Senate of the United States fifty years ago. And when we come to Taylor, what man who has an atom of love for California in his heart, that will not reverence the name of Taylor—the grand old hero of the Mexican war, the hero of Palo Alto, who opened the Halls of the Montezumas, threw down the walls of the City of Mexico, and gave us California—God bless her!—the sweetest, ripest, happiest commonwealth ever seen by humanity since Adam and Eve, hand in hand, walked out of the Garden of Paradise under the curse of Almighty God.

We give you, then, Clay Webster Taylor. He sprang from the people; he belongs to the people; let us give him back to them; we can give them no better man; he is their idol, their champion, their offspring; and before God, Mr. Chairman, I do not believe the people will repudiate him.

LECTURE REPORTING.

KEY TO NOTES COMMENCING ON PAGE 228.

A LECTURE ON DARWIN AND DARWINISM, BY THE REV. DR. STEBBINS, AT THE INDEPENDENT CHURCH, OAKLAND, TUESDAY EVENING, JUNE 7, 1881.

(Reported in full by the Author for the "Oakland Evening Tribune.")

He spoke as follows: My theme this evening is "Darwin and Darwinism." Within the last twenty-five years one of the most familiar names with thoughtful people has been the name of Charles Robert Darwin, the naturalist, and his name has become the synonym of a theory—a theory at once most brilliant and most profound—of the development of organized beings on this globe. In 1859 Darwin published his great work, "The Origin of Species"—a work that has attracted the attention of the civilized world, not only for the wonderful knowledge it displays of scientific facts, and great powers of generalization, but for the questions it raises and the profound controversy it excites, touching the relations of this world of living things, of mind and will. This world, somehow, seems to be imbedded in mind—somehow. How? is the question; and a theory that has got strength enough to raise that question starts the foundations of the universe. But theories are very theoretical, and the number of the theories of creation that have really got any intellectual hold at the center of things, may be compared with the number of successful patents as contrasted with the number of patent rights applied for. Theories all the way down from Plato to Spencer have been the playthings of the mind—nursery glass balls—as compared with those crystal spheres balanced in airy security through infinite space. But let me say a word about Darwin himself—the master of fine temper, of courtesy, of truth and imagination. Darwin is now a man seventy-two years old. He was descended from a line of naturalists as our Emerson was from a line of preachers. His grandfather was a physician, a botanist, and a poet. His poetical talent seems to have been kindled by his observations in nature among plants—his observations of a principle or germ which his illustrious grandson was destined to unfold into a universal law. As it happens, it was one hundred years ago (1781) Erasmus Darwin published a poem that he called the "Botanic Garden," in which he figures the loves and marriages of flowers and plants. With ingenious melody and subtle fancy he transmutes men and women into trees and flowers. (The lecturer here quoted from the poem.) Now these seeds of things and seeds of the theories of things, lay folded in the poetic mind of the ancestor—though dim and nebulous—to be gathered into shining centers of thought by him who should come after. But the father of Darwin was also a physician. He was one of those silent men—a man too deep and too strong to make a noise, and too self-respectful to try to be notorious. He educated his son at home and at school, and Darwin, at the age of twenty-one, volunteered as a naturalist on board of her Majesty's ship Beagle. The journal he kept is a very remarkable book, and has been called one of the most interesting books ever written. Before publishing the "Origin of Species" he had written several things that would have given him a reputation as a philosophical observer. But this "Origin of Species" was the result of twenty years' work—a noble pledge of intellectual honor. And since that great work he has published several others related directly or indirectly to that; and it may be said that Darwin is as fairly, as frankly, as firmly, and as unostentatiously before the world as any man that ever spoke to the scientific mind of any period. He has that untiring patience in accumulating and that wonderful skill in using large masses of facts—facts of the most variable and complex kind; that wide and accurate physiological knowledge; that acuteness in devising and skill in carrying out experiments; that remarkable style of composition—clear, persuasive, judicial, and courteous, which mark him best fitted, perhaps, of all men now living to bring this vast realm of unappropriated facts under the dominion of known laws. To this he has devoted himself with patient genius and with brilliant power. Now, in speaking of Darwinism as a theory, it is impossible not to speak of evolution, and it is to be borne in mind that, though they are intimately related, they are not identical. It is interesting to think how the seed of all our present modes of thought have been unfolded from the speculative views of the men of former time.

The doctrine of Development seems to have been included in David's reverent wonder concerning the origin of his being. David was a Darwinian. He was a philosopher without knowing it. "My substance was not hid from thee. When I was made in secret and curiously wrought in the lowest parts of the earth, thine eyes did see my substance yet being unperfect, and in thy book all my members were written which in continents were found, when as yet there were none of them." This is saying that creation has had a history; that man's experience on this earth has had a history; that it has not been a single act, but a long series of acts—a process of forever and perpetual encroaching of Divine power and work, continuously pursued through an inconceivable lapse of time. It is saying, also, that this work has been pursued in time and by method; that there is an observed order of facts which is carried on by law. Now, such conceptions as these are found here and there in continually increasing clearness and power through the entire history of human thought. Evolution, as I understand it, rests on the universally observed fact of progress in nature. This universe is not a stationary, accomplished, and concluded fact. This earth is not done yet; it is not finished, but an ever-working process—a process going on by method and in time. It is a term (evolution) about which there is a great deal of cant. It plays about the same part in the unscientific mind that what we call nasal piety does in the unspiritually religious. There are two ways of understanding anything. One way is to understand what it is—that is, to understand it. The other way is to understand what it is not. The first way is for specialists; the second way is for amateurs and bunglers —for me—and, perhaps, for yourselves. It is no part of my design to criticise the philosophy of evolution. That should be left to more competent specialists; and I shall not have the imprudence to say that I believe it, beyond the fact that in a great and general way it is a great and consistent theory of nature. Now, whatever those who are fitted for such work can do to develop the theory, whatever facts their well-trained mind and scientific spirit can bring out and establish, I shall be ready gratefully to own and accept; but that is not my province. It is not my province to expand the boundaries of human thought in this direction, certainly. I must content myself with the more respectful place and humbler knowledge of the amateur. I must content myself with what the theory is *not*, and thus I say Evolution, like the Christian religion, carries with it a great deal that does not belong to it. As a great general fact of nature, it is doubtless true—as true as it is grand; but if a man would have the full life and intelligence of it, he must have some other notion than that it is equal to everything, and everything is equal to it—that everything can be accounted for by evolution, and evolution can be accounted for by everything. Now, I suppose, first of all, in regard to the doctrine of evolution—I suppose that anything to be evolved must first be involved. If you would get anything out of anything, it must first be in something. I suppose that making anything by hand or machine, as a pair of shoes or a house, is not evolution. In most of the cases in which the term is used it does not really signify what is intended by it. For instance, the nebular theory of the universe—the theory that worlds were formed from nebulous matter and gathered into bodies. But the process by which suns and planets were formed was involution, the opposite of evolution. It was winding up, instead of unwinding. The change of society from barbarism to civilization is sometimes called evolution instead of education. They are accretion. They are no more evolution than the barnacles on a ship are evolution from the ship. There can be no evolution without previous involution. That is the great bottom fact. Now, the doctrine of evolution is known as Darwinism, though it does not originate with Darwin. The derivation of vegetable and animal kinds from single archetypes, through a set line of forms—there is an evolution there which is an unrolling of a world plan. That world plan is not yet fully presented in any theory of evolution. It is too early to predict the future of the theory with certainty,

On the one hand there are strong probabilities in its favor; on the other hand it is to be proved. It must be found to harmonize, so as to command the suffrages of the whole scientific world. Now, Darwinism is based on the doctrine of evolution, and is that particular application of it which excites a peculiar interest because it teaches the origin of man. It was the notion, formerly, that this earth was a fixity, absolute and permanent, and the announcement that it turned was a shock to all human thought. It was the common opinion of men, until a comparatively recent day, that species of plants and animals were a fixity—that each species was created by a direct creative power, and pursued its way an unmingled and unmingling stream. Darwin affirms that this is not a true account or conception of the relation of organized beings on the earth. Now, it is well known that man can, by pursuing a certain method of breeding or cultivation, improve, and, in different ways, modify the character of the different domestic animals and plants. Darwin says that they are also found in the conditions and circumstances of nature—that is, he holds that man, in the application of his intelligence to the variation and improvement of species, is only copying from nature and doing what nature is doing perpetually by her own laws. Now, the kernel of Darwin's creed is this: "I can entertain no doubt, after the most deliberate study, that the view which most naturalists entertain, and which I formerly entertained, namely, that each species has been independently created, is erroneous. I am fully convinced that species are not immutable, but that those which belong to the same genera are really descended from the same species. I am convinced that natural selection has been the main, but not the exclusive means of modification." Now, here is the grand proposition or declaration of variability of species, and how the variations have been made. I suppose that the doctrine of the fixity of species is now abandoned, just as surely as the doctrine of the fixity of this earth is abandoned. That doctrine died a royal death with Agassiz. The means of variation is what Darwin calls natural selection. Now, this enunciation of a principle or law in the development of plants and animals, is equaled only in brilliancy and power by Newton's conception of the law of gravitation. It may be said, perhaps, by some, that the generalization of Darwin surpasses in brilliancy of imagination the original conception of Newton. Now, how far does the great naturalist carry it? "I cannot doubt," he says, "that the theory of descent by modification embraces all the members of the same class, and I believe all animals have descended from at most only four or five progenitors, and plants from an equal or a lesser number." And then here is the conclusion. "Probably all the organic beings which have ever lived on this earth have descended from some primordial form into which life was first breathed." The interest that this theory has awakened may be accounted for only by the fact that it displaces venerable traditions. It is very interesting for us to know our ancestors. Darwin's theory includes man among animals. The creation is not an accomplished fact or a supreme fiat, but an unending process, every step of which displays the presence and unity of the great universal power and cause. Now, it is not my purpose to raise the theological argument; that is another inquiry. How things are done, not who did them: how change has been made in the ranks of organized beings, not what power or cause made that change; how man as an animal has appeared on this earth, not whether he is a spiritual being. Science is concerned with method, not with cause. It is the duty of a scientific man, as a scientific man, to report what he finds among tangible things, and that is all. And while it is his duty to exclude other things, that does not imply any contempt for the other things. It is the duty of a scientific man to exclude spiritual things. Then, if I may say so, it is his duty to exclude God. And thus, and here, without lugging in anything that is foreign or afar, let me only say that you will search Darwin's books in vain for a single irreverent utterance. The same may be said of one of our own American world-renowned naturalists (Gray), who has from the first kept equal pace with Darwin, and has elaborated concurrently with him, rather than received from him, the theories that bear his name. But this is by the way only. Theories have been constructed and engrafted into Darwinism which must stand or fall by their own merit, and Darwin has undertaken to carry out his theory into the sublime heights of man's being. He has pushed his sublime hypothesis to the very outer rim of the universe, and attempted to bridge the chasm between mind and matter, or between the highest animal and the lowest man. With admiring deference I hold the humble, yet firm and confident opinion, that on that shadowy twilight border-ground between the Me and the *not* Me—the conscious self of moral glory, where the armed knights move as sheeted ghosts, and sword cuts sword in viewless air, no Damascus-blade of polished physical fact can ever win. The full development and theory of the Darwinian hypothesis suggests that all are equal lineal descendants from some few beings who lived long before the first bed of the silurian system was deposited; and where does this put us? It puts us in the rank of living beings having a common origin. To characterize this by contemptuous satire, to speak of man as being descended from a monkey, is unjust and unscientific, and as absurd as to characterize the poetic conception of man's creation by direct divine power as being descended from mud and clay. They are both equally the caricature of sterile minds, feeble conception, and dull sensibility. I can conceive how a stupid bigot can put it in that way, but I cannot see how a man that lives, that loves truth, and thinks that truth has some origin as well as himself, and that he himself is a part of that truth, can find any expression or place for any chattering scorn about a theory. The man who believes in a Maker, I think, shows his good sense by leaving the making to the Maker. It stands thus, then. Species are not independent descendants in one line. That view has played its part, and sleeps in the wept and honored grave of Agassiz. If you would observe the facts yourselves, go among the domestic animals or into the kitchen garden, and find that no pure species and no unmixed race exists. Observe that the peach and nectarine are from the same stock. See how the cattle-breeder prunes, as the vine-trainer cuts his vines; and see what a conglomerate of all mankind this American people are. Now, this process of mixing and selecting, when carried on by man, is progress; it is improvement; it is growth; it is taking up what exists in nature already and carrying it forward. Thus, as commerce woos the winds of heaven into her sails, or as steam brings all the weight of the atmosphere upon her engines, and sends the train up and down the continent. The fact is that there is in nature a susceptibility, a capacity for these changes, and growths, and minglings. Darwin says that they have been going on in nature through unmeasured eons—now almost imperceptible, now by striking contrast. He calls it natural selection. When man does it, it is modification; it is improvement by adding man's intelligence to a natural law; but when nature does it—wild and untutored—it is a struggle for existence. Now, it is an interesting fact in the history of human thought, that Darwin's theory of natural selection is based on the philosophy of Hobbes and Malthus. Darwin applied to animals what those philosophers applied to man. Hobbes affirmed that the universe was at constant war; Malthus said that human population would so overrun production that the earth would be filled with famine. Hobbes' was a totally inadequate statement. The Malthusian theory of overpopulation was a mistake in regard to the human world, but it was a truth in regard to the animal world. The case may be plainly stated thus: Organized beings have an immense power of increase. Plants yield their crop of seeds annually, and most wild animals bring forth their young yearly. Now, if this should go on unchecked for a comparatively short period, the earth would be overrun. You have all heard the story of the blacksmith who agreed to shoe the farmer's horse, charging a cent for the first nail, two for the second, and so on. The farmer soon found that he had no need of the horse, as the farm had to be deeded away to smithy for shoeing the brute. Now, take fifty seeds of a plant; let them all grow. Next year there are twenty-five hundred, and so on. In nine years there will be a plant on every square foot of dry land on the surface of this globe. A pair of elephants —the slowest breeders of all animals, bringing forth three pairs in sixty years—would in the fifth century have a living progeny of fifteen millions. Now, we are interested in the population of our country. Thirty millions doubling once in twenty-five years, in a little less than seven hundred years would give a square foot to each one on the whole surface of the globe, land and water. Thus, the room of the earth is entirely inadequate to this vast increase, and food is limited. For instance, consider what can be done by the Fish Commissioners in this State. In the natural state, about two eggs out of a thousand come to maturity. By care, nine hundred and ninety young fishes can be preserved—an instance of the power of man to increase the means of subsistence that puts the Malthusian theory all out of the question. Malthus' theory is true, and starvation continues until man sets up his improvement. Hobbes' theory is true, and the whole world is thrown into war for existence. Nature chooses the best to survive, and this is carried on in a large way over wide areas of time. Through this selection of the best by the hard struggle for room and for food, the different organized beings—animals and plants—rise to higher and higher forms. This is a kind of Napoleonic doctrine, that Providence favors the strong battalions. It is true in some relations of men and things. Now, under this doctrine the past is very rough. If we could only let bygones be bygones, and begin anew and go on, the future prospect is pleasanter than the backward look. As we look into the early geologic ages the lines converge, and they point to conclusions inevitable. A step back and our relations are the Hottentots, the African bushmen. Reason makes no objection to that; pride may, and it may be a little taken down. When we go one step further to a closer aspect of our ancestors of the olden time, our poor relations of the four-handed family are suggested. It is to be confessed by all —noble lord and lovely lady—that the monkey does look too much like us to be quite agreeable, and his looking so much like us does suggest, to superficial knowledge and observation, the possibility of kinship; but let us not be too much chagrined at that. Let us think also what the monkeys might say; but science, and this theory based on science, surely does not move on those lines. The monkey is not next to us in the animal kingdom. The monkey is not so near man as the horse. There are many brute kinds that are nearer man than the anthropoids. Man, for instance, stands on two feet, and that is the foundation he stands on as his own. The thumbs on a monkey's foot are just as much in the way, scientifically, as a horse's hoof. The thumbs on a monkey's foot put him further from man than the hoof on a horse puts the horse from a man. Put the genealogy of the brute where you will, but the four-handed races are not our forerunners; and unless some monkey—live or fossil—is found, with a good, honest great-toe instead of a thumb, there is good ground for believing that man may stand for himself yet awhile as a separate creation, however it may be with the lower. And this theory of relation and selection may play its part, and so may specific creation. But somebody will say, "Why all this fuss? Why all this new theory, anyway? What matters it? Let the world go on. Let it alone. Why not hold fast to the customary view that all species were directly created after their respective kinds? Why this continual striving after the dim and the unattained and the unaccountable?

Why this anxious endeavor of scientific men and of philosophers to penetrate into the mysterious?" Now, the general answer may be found in the activity of the human intellect and the delirious and divine desire to know, stimulated as it has been by its own success, in the fact that the principal triumphs of our age in physical science have consisted in tracing connections where none were known before, in reducing mixed phenomena to a common cause or origin. This is the line of scientific research and the line of scientific triumph and success. Now, can the mind of the age be expected to let this question be about species which lies directly in the line of its great traces—can it be expected to let that pass? It will raise the question why animals began to be as they are, and where they are; and it will never admit that the inquiry is beyond its reach until all endeavor fails. And here is a mass of disjointed facts. The mind resents it as nature abhors a vacuum. All origin is with the originator. The question is, whether we have got back to the origin. The mind, inspired with the enthusiasm of truth, will inquire into the order of the phenomena. You might as well expect your child to grow up with the extent of what he is told about the advent of his little baby brother. To learn that the little new-comer is the gift of God only stimulates inquiry. The questioning philosopher in short clothes is the father of the man. Whatever the Almighty Maker has done, man will ask, and he will rush into the Divine Presence and ask, How did you do it? This is the spirit of man when awakened; it is the God-like spirit in man. Now, there is a question that Darwinism raises, and which lies in the minds of intelligent persons, and which modifies their thought—Was man originally savage, and thence elevated into civilization; or was he gifted with such knowledge as prepared him for refined life? Now, the theory of Darwin does not answer that question, neither does it attempt to answer it. Darwin's attempt to carry his theory up into the higher place of man would lead us to infer that man was a rudimentary being when he first appeared upon the earth. We are not compelled to accept that by the theory. History shows barbaric degeneration to have been the rule, with partial revivals and expansions here and there. There is no proven instance of any nation or race having initiated its own advancement out of barbarism, while there are many examples of the deterioration of powerful empires and centers of magnificent culture into a savage, or almost savage state. The historic fact is, always a force from without has begun the elevation of a race or community. When history has failed to reach such beginnings, tradition follows its clues toward them, and always with the same indication. Egypt got its beginnings from a cross with India. Greece got hers by mixing with Cadmus; Rome from Greece; Europe first imported from Rome, and then from Palestine. The testimony of history goes to show that man cannot develop himself. Now, Darwinism allows room and opportunities for elevation, for foreign influence; and there is nothing in the hypothesis that excludes the most abundant inspiration. Darwinism has an upward and onward look, and flings out its banner on every tower and citadel of the mind. It excites a profound interest in the minds and hearts of persons that would hardly confess it. Under its touch nature becomes a new, divine manifestation. It lifts from the shoulders of man the responsibility for the fact of death. Woman can no longer be taunted with having brought down on herself the pangs that make her sex a martyrdom. If development upward is the general law of the race, we have everything to hope for and everything to believe in in the future. And that the question can be discussed without offense, shows that we are entering upon a new era—a revival greater than the revival of letters—the revival of humanity.

SERMON REPORTING.

KEY TO NOTES COMMENCING ON PAGE 242.

Extracts from a Sermon by the Rev. L. Hamilton, at the Independent Church, Oakland, Sunday, Aug. 28, 1881.

(Reported by the Author.)

Seventh chapter of Matthew, sixteenth verse. "Do men gather grapes of thorns, or figs of thistles?"

No. You must prune the rose if you would pluck it. You must sow for the harvest you reap. Experience tells you what to expect. The laws of God never play fast and loose.

Apply this now to human character, and it is what I have sown—what I am sowing—which will make my future character. It is a basis thought of any religion, or of any morality. The heaven and hell of our childhood are both dispelled illusions. We no longer hope for the one, nor fear the other. We have come to see that the one is a burlesque on happiness, the other a blot on the character of God. What is to take their places?

I believe there are solid reasons. I believe that the common man may be made to see them, and to feel their force. I believe they furnish a substitute that can be put in the place of them. I want to make the substitute plain to-day.

I am often reproached with being too philosophical. I am told that the people cannot understand my over-refined reasons and reasoning, and that I must coax them into being good, and encourage fear to reason them out of being bad.

I don't believe it. I don't believe there was a child ten years old in your Sunday-school this morning, or in any other Sunday-school, that needs the one or the other. Children do need, undoubtedly, parental authority and restraint—sometimes what we used to call "smart medicine, rubbed on"—but do not need that monstrous fiction of the future, which has turned the nights of millions of children into a long, sleepless terror. Children do need the love and fostering care of parents to make a heaven for them now, and start them well on their way to any better heaven that may appear in the future, but do not need that "harping" that has been named heaven. And I do not believe there is an unlettered Irishman that couldn't be made to understand and feel the real reasons for doing right to others and respecting himself with better moral effect from it than comes from the fiction of the future life; and when we take half the pains to teach him the reasons that we now take to teach him the fictions, the reality can be made a great deal more permanent in its influence than the myths or ghosts.

Let us come to the substitute. I will first express it in a word. It is the simple fact that the soul is an organic life. The soul is an organic life, and this fact once comprehended in its length and breadth and height and depth, will have more influence to keep men from all wrong and move them to all right, than all the hells and heavens that barbaric ignorance ever invented. The soul is an organized being, existence, or life, that lives and grows under the law of all organic life—retains its identity, is full of health, vitality, and joy, if cared for according to the laws of its nature, and dwarfed and filled with pain and misery if those laws are violated ; grows in the former case ; ends in blasting and withered disappointment in the latter. * * * * *

Now, hearers, this is what I would substitute for the fictitious heaven and hell of theology—this idea of the soul growing and shaping itself under the laws of all organic life.

Here is where I differ so with the teachings of the Church. I charge —and I do this, friends, in no spirit of iconoclasm ; I do it because I feel that it must be done before a way is prepared for a better progress of humanity—I charge these teachings of the Church with corrupting the morals of Christendom : giving out the idea, as they do, that character can be suddenly changed or recreated at the will of another; that sin and its due punishment can be arbitrarily remitted on the merit of another ; that an atonement for sin has been made which is able to send the vilest criminal of earth straight from the gallows into heaven—it is a monstrous fiction. It has worked decay and corruption through and through the masses, till, if you will go to the vilest quarters of our cities, and search closely into the swarms that swelter and rot, you will find their minds saturated by the idea that their vile past can be made pure. That thought has penetrated those masses wherever I have met them. They are almost all religious ; and they believe in the atonement of the Church and the grace of God, and they sin on the force of it. It is not the dreadful dogmas of the Church that do most harm. It is their sentimental Gospel. We must strike right at that—the ideal of life they give, the ideal of character they set up, the very sum and substance of what they call the truth—*it is rotten to the core! it is false!* It is a fictitious salvation from a fictitious hell to a fictitious heaven. It makes a virtuous fiction out of the lives of men and women who are striving for this salvation, in a large degree. We must get out of it before we can get into reality. And it needs another Luther, I think, to expose this corruption. Then we will have the real word of Jesus—one interpretation of character shaped by eternal law.

I think, friends, that idea will take stronger hold on man as a motive power than the old-fashioned terror. It comes right home every moment—the being I am taking on; what I do goes into the very blood and is shaping what I am to be. * * * * * * *

Look closely into the idea of God; the idea of his enemy also, the devil—ideas which you project into the invisible world with your own mind—and all terrors vanish. God is your friend. He will do the very best for you that you will let him do. The devil cannot hurt you unless you choose to let him have a hold on you. There is nothing from the unseen world for you to fear—nothing to be feared that you do not carry along with you. I would I could describe to you the inspiration, the hope, the noble endeavor, that will follow from this liberty. There is not time. But each one may say the kind of soul he will grow to be, as he pictures that beauty and perfection which Christ has left—which the idea that ever works at the human mind is forever limning before the noble and the true—the glory of the perfect growth that he may wear. Out of this poor animal existence in which I begin, toward that life of eternal reality of thought, love, aspiration, realization; out of this weakness toward that power; out of this fickle life of passion toward that peace; out of this littleness into that greatness; out of these conscious defects into that divine perfection. The shining path, with steps laid firm in eternal law, stretches for my feet onward towards its possession. Rise and away, that every step, prompt and firm, moment by moment, carry me toward the prize.

PRAYER.

O God, may we catch the inspiration of that ideal being which thou hast placed before us, and made attainable by us! May the young feel the possibilities that are open to them, and O, may they not trample upon the laws of their being and their growth! Make them earnest, cheerful, joyful, thoughtful of the issues that depend upon the manner in which they spend the day that is passing, and may all that they do add to the growth which tends to make them divine in virtue and truth. Amen.

VOCABULARY.

211. The following copious list of words and phrases, together with those given in the previous pages, contains nearly all the forms which the writer will ever need, and furnishes abundant analogies for the few words for which he may be obliged to extemporize outlines.

Following the Vocabulary proper will be found lists giving the correct forms for the Months, Days of the Week, Names of Countries, States and Territories, Cities and Towns, Miscellaneous Phrases, Business Phrases and Forms, and Law Phrases and Forms.

While the Vocabulary proper is intended for reference in case of doubt as to the proper outline, the lists commencing with the months it will be well to write repeatedly from dictation until familiarized. This is specially important with regard to the lists of phrases, which should be learned as thoroughly as the forms for any other contractions, if the writer would get the practical benefit which may be derived from them.

The forms assigned to words designated by an asterisk should be strictly adhered to and specially noted, as they are devised to secure the writer against conflict between words which would naturally be written with the same outline.

In devising forms, the importance of the law of analogy has been borne in mind, and its requirements have been observed as far as is consistent with the variation of outline necessary to prevent conflict between words.

The words are arranged alphabetically, and the shorthand outlines indicated by their stenotypes in a very satisfactory manner, the availability of this method rendering it possible to give a much larger list than would otherwise be practicable.

A hyphen connects syllables forming derivatives, with the primitive word, showing that the shorthand outline indicated by the stenotypes stands for either; so derivatives will occasionally be found in the alphabetical place of the primitive, their outlines taking the same position.

In forming contractions, any adverb formed by the addition of the syllable *ly* to the adjective may be represented by the same form as the adjective, and generally the same form may be used for the noun, verb, adjective, and adverb. If there are two or more derivative nouns from the same primitive, care must be taken to provide distinctive forms for them.

Small superior figures printed after a stenotype indicate the position of the shorthand sign, whether First, Second, or Third. All the words given in this Vocabulary are intended to be written in position according to the accented vowel, unless specially directed to the contrary, and these particular cases will usually be the only ones in which the position will be indicated by superior figures.

Words in quotation marks refer to the previous list of word-signs.

RECAPITULATION OF STENOTYPY.

212. For convenience of reference, a review of Stenotypy is here given, together with illustrations of all the principles of contraction in the system, with their stenotypes adjacent.

sP	Ptrt	Pstr	Pft
sL	Pshnt	Pntr	Ilw
nP	Pss	Pshn	wL
strP	Pns	Pnshn	wP
Ps	Ptrs	Pr	sPr
Pn	Pshns	Pl	sPl
Ptr	Psts	lP	sNr
Pshn	Pnts	Pl	Pts
stP	Ptrts	Pt	Pfs
Pst	Pshnts	Pf	Nts
Pnt	Pnss	Ptl	Ptshn

All the stem letters are represented by Roman capitals, except when struck opposite to the alphabetic direction, they are indicated by italic capitals. All the adjuncts, such as hooks, circles, loops, etc., are represented by small Roman letters, except when, for the purpose of some special distinction, they are indicated by lower-case italics. (For the Vowel Stenotypy see Plate on page 24.)

A hyphen indicates nearness; a colon, the pointing in of vowels; and a semicolon, striking through a stem, whether consonants or vowels. c is the stenotype for the connecting hook, and e for the *con*, or the *ing* dot.

A lower-case u, d, r, or l, in parenthesis (u), (d), (r), (l), indicates that the form whose stenotype immediately precedes it should be struck up, down, right, or left, respectively; or, if that form is a half-circle, indicates the direction toward which the half-circle should open. f or b, in parenthesis (f), (b), indicates that a hook or circle on the stem whose stenotype immediately precedes, should be struck with Forward or Backward Motion.

LIST OF WORDS.

A

A	e^2	Abscond	BsKnt
Abandon	BnDn	Absence	BsNs
Abate	aBt	Absentee	BsNdE
Abbreviate	BrVt	Absolute	BsLd
Abbreviation	BrVshn	Absolve	BSlf
Abdicate	aBtKT	Absorb	Bs$R$$B$
Abdomen	aBtMn	Absorption	BsRPshn
Abdominal	aBtMNl	Abstain	BsTn
Abduce	Btus	Abstemious	BsTcMs
Abduction	BtKshn	Abstinent	BsNNd
Aberration	BRshn	Abstract-ly	BsT
Abeyance	BNs	Abstraction	BsTshn
Abhor	BHr	Abstruse	BsTus
Abide	aBt	Absurd	BsRd
Ability	BLT	Absurdity	BsRT
Abject	BJK	Abundance	BnNs
Able	Bl	Abundant-ly	BnNd
Able bodied	BlBtt	Academy-ic	KDcM
Abnormal	BnRMl	Accede	KsD
Aboard	BRd	Accelerate	KsLR
Abode	aBt	Access	KSs
Abolish	BlSh	Acclivity	Klf$E$T
Abolition	BlShn	Accommodate	KmDt
Abolitionist	BlShnS	Accompany	KN
Abominate-ion-ble-y	BMN	Accomplice	KmPLs
Aboriginal	BRJ	Accomplish-ment	KmPSh
Abortion	BRshn	According-ly-to	KD
About	B^3	Accouterments	KTRMs
Abrade	ABrt	*Accretion	AKrshn
Abridge	BrJ	Accrue	AKr
Abroad	Brt	Accumulate-ion	KuL
Abrogate	BRG	Accuracy	KRS
Abrupt-ly	BRP	Accurate-ly	KRd
Abscess	BSs	Accustom	KsM
		Ace	As

Acerbity	Sr*B*T	Admissible	DmsB
Acknowledge-ment	KnJ	Admission	Dmshr.
Acorn	AKrn	Admit	DmT
Acquaint-ed-ance	Knt	Admixture	DmKsChR
Acquiesce	KWs	Admonish	DmNSh
Acquire-ment	KW	Admonition	DmNShn
Acquisition	KWsShn	Adroit	Drt:awi
Acquisitive	KWsV	Adulation	Ju*L*
Acquit	KT	Adult	D*L*d
*Acre	AKr	*Adulterate-y	D*L*R
Acrid	*A*Krt	Advance	DfNs
Acrimony	*A*KrmN	Advantage	J^3
Across	Krs	Advantageous-ly	J^{3}s
Act	KT	Adventure	DfNChr
Active-ity	KTf	Adversary	D*V*rsR
*Actor	Keu	Advertise	Ds^2
Actuate	KChT	Advertisement	DsM
Addendum	DnDcM	*Advice-se	D^{3}fs
*Addition-al	D^{3}shn	Advisable	D^{1}sB
*Address	D^{3}rs	Advisedly	Dfst*L*
Adduce	Dus	Advisement	DfsM
Adequate	DK1T	Adviser	Dfs*R*
Adhere	DHr	Advocacy	DfKS
Adhesion	DcHshn	Aeriform	A*RF*r
Adieu	Du	Aeronaut	A*R*Nd
Adjournment	JrnM	Afar	*A*Fr
*Adjudicate	JDK	Affect	*F*K
Adjunct	JnKT	Affectation	*F*KTshn
Adjustment	JsM	Affiance	*F*Ns
Admeasurement	DcMZh	Affidavit	FV
Administer	Ds*R*	Affinity	*F*nT
Administration	DsRshn	Affirm-ative	F*R*M
Administrator	DsR*R*	Afflict	*F*lK
Administratrix	DsR*R*Ks	Affluent	*F*lNd
Admirable-y	DMrB	Afford	*F*R
Admire-ation	D^{1}Mr	Affront	*F*rnt
Admirer	DMrR	Aforesaid	FrSt

After	F^s	Analogous	NloGs
Afternoon	F^{s}nN	Analogy	NloJ
Afterwards	F*R*ts	Analysis	NlSs
Against	Gst	Analytic	NltK
Agent	JN	Analyze	NlZ
Ago	G^s	Anatomy	NtM
Agriculture-al	G^{s}r K*l*	*Ancestor	NsStr
Agriculturist	GrK*l*st	*Ancestry	NsStR
Ailment	AlM	Anchor	NKr
Alderman	L*R*Mn	Ancient	NShnt
Alert	L*R*d	And	e^s
Alienate	LNd	Anecdote	nKDt
All	*l*^{i}(u)	Aneurism	NYRsM
Alleviate	LVt	Angel	NJl
Allure	L*R*	Anger-y	Ng*R*
Almighty	"all" MT	Angle	Ng*l*
Almost	"all" Mst	Angular	NgLR
Alphabet	LBt	Animal	NMl
Already	"all" *R*	Annexation	nKsAShn
*Also	"all" s	Annihilate	NL(f)d
Alter	L*R*	Anniversary	NVrsR
Alteration	L*R*shn	Announce	NNs
Altercation	L*R*Kshn	Annoyance	NNs
Alternate-ive	L*R*N	Annual-ly	N*l*(u)
Although	"all" Dh	Another	"another"
Altitude	LTTt	Answer	Ns*R*
Altogether	*l*(d)G^s	*Antagonist-ic	NtG
Always	"all" Z^s	Antagonism	NtGsM
Ambidextrous	MBtKstRs	Antarctic	N*R*KK
Ameliorate	AMlR	*Anterior	nT^{s}RR
Amendment	MnM	Anthracite	NThrSt
Amenity	MNT	Anticipate	nTsPt
Among	Ng^s	Antidote	nTDt
Amphibious	Mc*F*Bs	Antimony	NtMN
Amphitheater	McFThtr	Antipodes	nTPtis
Amplitude	MPtD	Antiquary	NtKR
An	e^s	Antique	NtK

Antiquity	NtKT	*Approbation	PBshn
Anxiety	NgsIT	Appropriate-ion	PP
Aorta	ART	*Approve	aPf
Apart	Pt	Appurtenance	PtNNs
Apathetic	PThtK	Aqueous	AKlS
Apex	APKs	Arbitrary	RBtRR
Apology	PLJ	Architect	RKK
Apologue	PlG	Architecture-al	RKChr
Apoplexy	PPKS	Arctic	RKK
*Apostle	aPsl	Arduous	RJs
Apothecary	PThKr	Area	AR
Appall	aPl	Arid	ARD
Apparatus	PRTs	Aristocracy	RstKS
Apparel	PRl	Aristocrat	RstKT
Apparent-ly	PnT	Aristocratic	RstKK
Appeal	Pl	Arithmetic-al	RThM
Appear	Pr	*Arm	Rm
Appearance	Prns	*Army	RM
Appendage	aPnJ	*Aroma	RMA
Appendix	PntKs	Arraign	Rn
*Appertain	PTn	Arrange	RnJ
Appetite	PTt	Arrest	RsT
*Apple	Pl	Arrive-al	Rv
*Appliance	Pl³Ns	Arsenic	RsNiK
*Applicable-ility	Pl³B	Art	RT
Applicant	Pl³Knt	*Article	RK
*Apply	Pl³	Articulation	RTKlshn
*Appoint	aPnt	Artifice	RFs
*Apportion	aPshn	Artificial	RFSh
*Apportionment	aPshnM	As	s³
*Appraise	APrs	Ascendant	SnNt
Appreciate	PrSht	Ascendancy	SnNS
*Apprehend	Pr³nD	Ascension	SnShn
*Apprehensible	Pr³nsB	Ascertain	SrtN
*Apprehension	Pr³nshn	*Asleep	SlP
*Apprehensive	Pr³sV	Aspect	SP
*Apprize	Prs:I	Asperity	SPrti

Aspire-ation	S*PR*	Aurora Borealis	*RRBRL*s
Assail	S*l*	Auspicious	SPShs
Assault	S*l*t	Authentic-ate-ity	Thnt
*Assemblage	SMBJ	*Author	Thr
*Assembly	Sm*B*	Authoritative	Th*R*Tf
Assert	Srt	Authority	Th*R*T
*Assign	S³n	Autocrat	awTKrT
*Assist-ance	S³st	Automatic	awT-M
*Assistant	S³sNt	*Autumn	awTm
Associate	SSht	Auxiliary	Ks*LR*
Assort	Srt	*Available	V*l*B
Assuage	ScJ	Avarice	*V*Rs
Assurance	Shrns	Avenge	*V*nJ
Astonish-ment	StN	Aver	*A*Vr
*At	T³	Averse	*A*Vrs
*Atheist	Thst	Avocation	*V*³Kshn
*Atheistical	Thst*i*	*Avoid	*V*D
Atmosphere-ic	Ts*F*	Avoidance	*V*Dns
*Atom	aTm	Avoirdupois	*V*rDPs
Attach	TCh	Aware	W³
Attachment	TChM	Awful	awFl
Attempt	TmP*t*	Awkward	KRd
*Attention	Tshn	Aye	A*i*
Attenuate	TnT		
*Attenuation	TnAShn	**B**	
*Attract	Tr³	Backward	BK*w*R
*Attraction	Tr³shn	Backwoods	BK*w*Ds
*Attractive	Tr³Tf	Baker	BKR
Auburn	awBrn	Bakery	BKR*i*
Auction	Kshn	Balance	Blns
Auctioneer	Ks*NR*	*Ballot	B*L*d
*Audience	awDns	Ballot-box	BBKs
*Auditor	awDtr	Bandage	BnJ
*Auditory	awDR	Banish	*B*nSh
August	Gst	Bankrupt	BnKP
Aureolar	aw*RL*	Banquet	BK*l*T
Auricle	*R*K*l*	Baptism	B*P*

Baptist	B*P*st	Birthright	*B*RTht
Barbarian	Br*B*n	Bishop	BSh
Barbarity	B*BT*	Bloodthirsty	BltThst*i*
Barometer	BrmTR	Body	Bt¹
Barouche	BRSh	Bolster	B*l*(u)st*R*
Bath	*B*Th	Bony	BoN
Bayonet	BoN	Both	*B*Th
*Beatify	BtF	Breakfast	Br*F*st
Beautiful	Bt*F*l	Breath	*B*rTh
*Beautify	Bt*F*	*Bright	Br*IT*
Beauty	Bti	Brilliant	BrYnt
*Became	BKM	Brother	Brtr
Because	Ks¹	Brotherhood	BrHd
*Become	BK	Bulk	B*L*K
Beelzebub	B*l*(u)s*B*	*Bullet	B*l*T
*Behin	Hnt¹	Buoyant	BYnt
Being	BNg	Burden	BrtN
*Belief-ve	Blf	*Burn	Brn
*Belong	BlNg	*Burst	B*R*st
Beneath	*B*nTh	Busybody	BsBti
*Beneficent	Bn*F*sNd	But	"But"
*Beneficial	Bn*F*	Butterfly	Bt*F*lI
Benefit	Bn*F*T	By-word	B*wR*t
*Benevolence-t	Bn*V*		
Bequeath	BKl	**C**	
Berth	*B*RTh	*Cajole	KAJl
Betake	BtK	Calculate-ion	Kl*L*
Better	Btr	Calendar	KlntR
Between	T¹	Call	K*l*
Beware	BWr	Calvary	K*lV*r
Bewilder	Bw*LR*	*Came	KM
Bewitch	Be*w*Ch	Camphene	Km*F*n
*Beyond	Bnt¹	*Can	K³
Bias	BS	Canal	KN*l*
*Bible	B*B*	Canary	KN*R*
Billiards	BlYs	Cancellation	KNsShn
Billion	BlYn	Cancer	KnsR

Candidate	KntDt	Cattle	Kt*l*
Canker	KnKR	Caudal	KD*l*
Cannibal	KNB*l*	Causation	KsAShn
Cannon	KNN	Cauterize	KTIs
Cannonade	KNNd	Cavalier	K*V*lR
*Cannot	KnT	Cavalry	K*V*lR*i*
*Canopy	KNP	Cavity	K*tET*
Canvas	Kn*V*s	Celebrate-d	Sl*B*
Canvass	Kn*V*s	Celebrity	Sl*BT*
Capitulate	KPChlT	Celerity	Sl*RT*
*Capricious	KPiShs	Celestial	SlSh
Captivate-ty	KPfT	Celibacy	s*L*BS
Captive	KPf	Cellar	Sl*R*
Car	KR	Cellular	SlLR
Carbon	KrBn	Celluloid	SlLt
Card	KRd	Censure	sNSh
Cardinal	KRdN*l*	Census	SnSs
*Care	Kr	Central	sNTr*l*
Career	KR*R*	Centralization	sNTrsAShn
Cargo	KrG	Center	sNtr
Caricature	KrKChr	Centrifugal	sNTrfG
Carnival	KRNVl	Centripetal	sNTrPt*L*
Carotid	KRawTt	Century	sNChr
Carpet	KrPt	Ceremony	s*Rm*N
Carriage	KRJ	*Certain-ly-ty	s*R*T
Cartridge	KRRJ	Certify-icate	SrtF
Cashier	KShr	Cervical	SrfK
Cashmere	KasMR	*Cessation	SsShn
Casual	KZhl	*Cession	Sshn
Catalogue	K*l*G	Chair	Chr
Catechise	Kt*E*Ks	Challenge	ChlnJ
Category	Kt*E*GR	Chamber	ChMB
Caterpillar	KTP*LR*	Champagne	Shm*P*n
Cathartic	KThrTK	Champion	ChMPn
Cathedral	KThDr*l*	Chancellor	Chns*l*R
Catholic	KThl	Chancery	ChnsR
Catholicism	KThlsM	Change	Ch³

Character	KK	Civilize	sVs
Characteristic	KKsK	Civilized	sVst
Characterize	KKIs	Claimant	KlMnt
Charge	Ch³	Clarionet	KlRN
Charity	ChrT	Clavicle	KltEK
Charlatan	Shrl(d)Tn	Clear-ly	KlR
Charnel-house	ChRNlHs	Clergy	KlRJ
Chattel	Chtl	Clergyman	KlRMn
Cheer	Chr	*Clerk	KlRK
Chieftain	ChTn	Client	KlN
*Child	Chl¹	Coalesce	KALs
Childhood	ChlD	Codify	KtF
*Children	Chln	Co-equal	KiKl
Chivalry	ShVlR	Co-eternal	KiTrn
Chloroform	KlRFrM	Co-exist	KKSst
Choir	KwR	Coffee	KtE
Christian	KrsChn	Coffin	KfEN
Christendom	KrsNM	Cogitate	KcJTt
Christmas	KrsMs	Cohabit	KcHB
Church	ChrCh	Coherent	KHrnt
Cicatrice-ze	sKATrs	Collect	KlK
*Circle	sRK	College	KlJ
*Circular	sRKR	Colonization	KlNsSbn
Circulate	sRKT	Color	KlR
Circulation	sRKshn	Colossus	KLsS
Circumference	SrFrns	Column	KLM
Circumlocution	sRlKshn	Combination	B¹nshn
Circumnavigate	sRNfG	Combustion	BsChn
Circumscribe	sRsKB	*Come	K²
Circumspect	sRsPK	Comedy	KMD
Circumstance	sTns	Comet	KMT
Circumstantial	sTSh	*Comfort-able	FRT
Cistern	SstRN	Command	e-Nd³
Citadel	sTDl	Commemorate-ive	e-MMRt
Citizen	sTsN	Commendable	NdABl
Civil	sV	Commendation	NdAShn
Civility	sVET	Commentary	NtAR

Commentator	NtA*eu*	*Comprehension	Pr¹nshn
Commerce	KMrs	*Comprehensive-ness	Pr¹s *V*
Commercial	KMr	*Compress	Pr¹s
Commiseration	KMsRshn	Compromise	KmPMs
*Commission	Sbn¹	Compulsion	P*l*(u)Shn
Commissioner	Shn*R*	Compunction	PnKshn
*Commit-tee	KmT	Computation	PtAShn
Common	K¹	Comrade	KmRd
Commonplace	K¹Ps:A	Concave	KnKf
Communicate	YnK	Concavity	KnKf*ET*
*Communion	Yn¹N	Conceal	*e*-s*L*
*Community	Yn¹T	Concede	*e*-sD
Companion	PnN	Conceit	*e*-St
Company	KN	Conceivable	SfAB
Comparable	P*R*B	Conceive	*e*-Sf
Comparative	P*R*Tf	Concentrate	sNTrt
Comparison	P*R*sN	Conception	sPshn
Compartment	KmPtM	Concern-ing	Srn
Compass	KmPs	Concert	Srt
Compassion	KmPshn	Concertina	SrtN
Compatible-y-ility	PtB	Concession	S¹shn
Compensate	PnsT	Conciliate	s*L*T
Compensation	PsAShn	Conclude	*e*-Kl
Competent	PtNd	Concomitant	KnKTnt
Competition	Ptshn	Concussion	KnKshn
Competitor	Pteu	*Condemn	KntM
Compilation	P*l*(u)AShn	*Condemnation	KnMnShn
Complexion	PlKshn	Condensation	DsAShn
Compliance	PlNs	Condescend	D¹sNd
Compliant	PlNd	Condescension	D¹sNshn
Complicate	PlKT	*Condition-al	D¹shn
*Complication	PlKAShn	Conduct	D¹K
Comport	P*R*T	Conductor	DKtr
Composition	*e*-Psshn	Confederacy	FtRS
Composure	PZh	Confederate	*e*-FtRt
*Comprehend	Pr¹nD	*Confer	*e*-F
*Comprehensible	Pr¹nsB	Conference	*e*-Fns

Confide	*F*D	Considerate	sD*R*
*Confirm	Fr¹M	Consideration	sD¹shn
Conflagration	*F*lGshn	Consign	Sn
Conflict	*F*lK	Consignee	ScN
*Conform	K*F*r	Consist	Sst
*Conformation	K*F*rshn	Consistent	SsNt
Congenial-ity	KnJN*l*(u)	Console	e-s*L*
Congenital	KnJnT*l*	Consolidate	s*L*Dt
Conglomerate	GlmRd	Consonant	sNNt
Congratulate	GrChlT	Conspicuous	sPKs
*Congregation-al	KnGshn	Conspiracy	sPS
Congregationalism	KnGsNsM	Conspirator	sPTr
Congress	Grs	Conspire	e-sP*R*
Congressional	Grshn	Constable	stB
Conjecture	JKChr	Constabulary	stB*LR*
Conjugate	JG	Constant	sTnt
Connect	e-K	Constancy	sTnS
Connive	e-V	Constellation	stLshn
Connoisseur	KNsY	Consternation	st*R*N
Connubial	KNB*l*(u)	Constipate	stPt
Conquer	KnKR	Constituency	stChNS
Conquest	KnKst	Constituent	stChN
Consanguinity	e-sNGlnT	Constitution-al	stT¹shn
Conscience	Shns	Constitutionality	stTs*L*T
Conscientious-ly	ShnShs	Constitutionalist	stTs*L*st
Conscious-ly	Shs	Constitutive	stChTf
Conscript	KnsKP	Construct-ion	strK
Consecrate	KnsK	Contact	e-TK
Consecutive-ly	KnsKTf	Contagious	TcJs
Consent	e-Snt	*Contain	Tn¹
Consequence	sKns	Contaminate-ion	T¹cMN
Consequent	sKnt	Contemplate-ion	TmP*L*
Consequential	sKNSh	Contemporaneous	TmP*R*Ns
Conservative	SrfV	Contempt	TmPt
Conservatory	SrfR	Content	T¹nt
Conserve	e-Srf	Contention	T¹nshn
Consider	sD	Contentious	T¹Shs

Contentment	T¹nM	Cork	KRK
Context	KntKst	*Corporal	KrP*Rl*
Contiguity	KntGT	*Corporeal	KrP*Ril*(u)
Continent	KntNNd	*Correct	Kr¹K
Contingency	TnJNS	Correspond-ent	KrsPnt
Continue-al-ly	KntN	Corrupt	KrPt
Continuity	KntNT	Council-sel	Ks*L*
Contort	*e*-TRd	Country	KntR
*Contract	Tr¹	County	KnT
*Contraction	Tr¹shn	Courage	KRJ
Contractor	Tr¹eu	Court	K²
Contradict	KntD	Courtesy	KrtS
Contradiction	KntDshn	Covenant	KfNNd
Contradictory	KntDR	Cover	Kf
Contradistinct-ion	KntDsNg	Coverture	KfChR
Contradistinguish	KntDst	Crazy	KrAZ
Contrary	KntRR	*Creation	Krshn
Contravene	KntR*V*n	*Creator	Kreu
Contravention	KntR*V*shn	Creature	KrChr
Contribute	KntBt	Credit	KrD
Contribution	KntBshn	Credulity	KrJlT
Contributor	KntB*eu*	Crevice	Krf*E*s
Controvert-sial-sy	Knt*V*r	Crime	Krm
Contumacious	KnTcMShs	Criminal	KrmN
Conundrum	KnNDrcM	Crimination	KrmNshn
Convalescent	VlSnt	Cross-examine-ation	KrsMn
Convene-ience	} Vn	*Crowd	Krt
Convenient-ly		Cube	KuB
Convention-al	Vshn	*Cudgel	KJl
Conversation-al	VrSshn	Culminate-ion	KlMN
Convict	*V*K	Cultivate	Klt*V*
Convivial	V*Vl*	*Cure	KuR
Convolution	*e*-Vlshn	*Curiosity	KRs*ti*
Co-ordinate	Kc*R*DnT	Curious	KRs
Co-partner	KPNr	Currency	KRnS
*Copy	KP*i*	Current	KRnt
Cord	KRd	Custom	KsM

134　　　　LIGHT-LINE SHORTHAND.

Customer	KsMR	Degenerate-ion	DJnR
Cutter	KTR	*Deify	DF:Ei
Cycle	sIKl	Delegate	DLG
Cylinder	Slnt$R$	Deliberate	DlBt
Czar	ZR	Delicate	DLK
Czarina	ZRN	Delicious	DlShs
Czarowitz	ZRTs	Delight	DlT
		Delightful	DlTf

D

		Delinquent	DlnKnt
*Damage	DmJ	Delinquency	DlnKS
*Damn	D³m	Deliver-y	Dl
*Damnation	DmNshn	Deliverance	Dlns
*Danger	DnJR	Democracy	DmKS
Dare	DR	Democrat-ic	DmK
*Dark	DRK	Demolish	DMlSh
*Daughter	Dtr	Demonstrate	DmsT
Dear	DR	Demoralize-ation	DMrl
*Decease	DsS	Demur	DMr
Decision	Dsshn	Demurrer	DMrR
Decisive	DSsV	Demure	DMr
Declaim-ation	DKlM	Denizen	DnsN
Declare-ation	DKlR	Denominate-ion	DnM
*Dedicate	DtKT	Denounce	DnNs
*Deduct	DtK	Density	DnsT
Defame	DfM	Deputy	DPti
Defaulter	DFltr	Derange-ment	DrnJ
Defeat	DtET	Derogate-ion-ory	DRG
Defect	DfK	Describe	DsKB
*Defence	Df	Description	DsKP
Defendant	D^s	*Deserve	DsR
Defensive	DfNSf	*Desiccation	DsKAShn
Defer	DFr	*Desire	DsR
Deficiency	DFsNS	Desist	DZst
Deficient-ly	DFsNd	*Desolate	DSlt
Definite	DfNd	Destroy-uctive	DstR
Deform	DFr	Destruction	DstRshn
Deformity	DFrT	Detach	DTCh

Deter	DTR	Disparage-ment	DsPJ
Determine-ation	DtM	*Disperse	DsPRs
Detonation	DtoNshn	*Displace	DsPls
Detract	DTr	*Disregard	DsRGr
Detraction	DTrshn	Disreputable	DsRPB
Develop-ment	DVl	Disrespect-ful	DsRsPK
Devil	DVl	Dissatisfy-action	DsTsF
*Devise	DVs	Dissimilar	DsM
Devolve	DVl	*Dissolute	DsLd
*Devote	DfoT	Dissolve	DSlf
*Devotion	DfosN	Dissuade	DSlt
Diameter	DmTR	*Distinct-ion	DsNg
*Differ-ence-ent	D^1	*Distinctive	DsNgf
*Difficult	Df^1	*Distinguish-ed	Dst
Dilapidate	DlPtT	Distract	DsT
*Dimension	DmNshn	Distribute	DstBt
*Diminish	DmNSh	Disturb	DstB
*Diminution	DmNShn	Disunion	DsNN
*Direct	DrK	*Disunite	DsNd:l
*Direction	Drshn	*Divide	DVt
Directly	DrKl	Dividend	DfEDnt
Director	Dreu	Divine	DfN
Directory	DrR	*Do	D^3
*Disadvantage	DsDfJ	*Doctor	Dr^1
Disagree	DsG	*Doctrine	Drn
Disbelieve	DsBl	*Dollar-s	D^1
Disciple	DsPl(u)	Domestic	DmsK
Discipline	DsPn	Domicile	DcMSl
Discover-y	DsKf	*Domination	DmNshn
Discoverer	DsKfR	Dominion	DmNN
Discredit	DsKD	*Doom	DuM
Discriminate-ion	DsKM	*Down	Dn^s
*Disease	DZs	*Downright	D^{3}nRd:l
*Disengage	DsNcG	*Downward	D^{3}nRd
Disinterested	DsNst$l$	Duet	DuT
Disloyal-ty	DsLl	Duplicate	DPK
Disoblige-ing	DsBJ	*Duration	Dr^{3}shn

136 LIGHT—LINE SHORTHAND.

During	Dr³	Employee	MPli
Dwarf	DlRv	*Enamel	NMl
Dwell-ing	Dl²	Encourage	nKRJ
Dwindle	Dlntl	Encyclopedia	NsKPta
		Energy	NRJ
E		*Engage-ment	nG
Each	Ch¹	English	NgSh
Early	Rl	Enlargement	nJ³
Earth	RTh	Enlighten	NltN
Earthquake	RThKlK	Entangle	NtNg
Eastern	Sn	Enterprise	NPs
*Ebony	BN	Enthusiasm-t-ic	nThsS
Ecclesiastic-al	KlZst	Entire-ly	NTr
Eclipse	iKlPs	Entwine	NTln
Economy	KnM	Entwist	NTlst
*Edition	EDshn	*Enviable	NVB
*Editor	Deu	*Epistle	Psl
*Educate-ion	JK	*Epoch	PK
Effect	FK	Equable-ility	iKlB
Effectual	FKChl	Equal	Kl
Efficacious	FKAShs	Equality	KlT
Efficiency	FShnS	Equalize	Klls
Efficient	FShnt	Equation	iKlshn
Eh	H:e	*Equator	iKl
Eject	JKT	Equivalent	KVlnt
Elaborate	LBt	Equivocate	KfoK
Elder	Ldr	Eradicate	RDK
Electioneer	LKsNR	Especial-ly	SP
Electric-ity	LK	Esquire	SKlR
Electrotype	LKP	Essential	SnSh
Emancipate	MsP	Establish-ment	SSh
Embellish-ment	MBSh	Estrange	STrnJ
Embrazure	MBZh	Eternal	Trn
Eminent	MNNt	Eternity	TrnT
Emolument	MlM	Eulogy	YJ
Emphasis-ze	McFsS	Euphony	YfoN
Emphatic	McF	Evade	EVt

LIGHT-LINE SHORTHAND.

Evangelist	VnJst	Execrable	KsKB
Even	EVn	Execute	KsKT
Event	Vnt	Executioner	KsKsNR
Eventual	VnChl	Executive	KsKTf
Ever	V¹	Executor	KsKeu
Everlasting	V¹lst	Executrix	KsKKs
Evermore	V¹M	Exegesis	KsJss
Every	V²	Exemplary	KsMPlR
Everywhere	V²R	Exemplification	KsMPFshn
Evidence	VD	Exempt	KsMPt
Evident	VDnt	Exercise	KsRsZ
Evolution	Vlshn	Exert	KsRd
Exact-ion	KsK	Exhale-ation	KsHl
Exalt	KsLd	Exhaust	KSst
Examine-ation	KsMn	Exhaustion	KSsShn
Example	KsMP	Exhibit	KsBt
Exasperate-ion	KSsP	Exhilarate-ion	K¹sLR
Excavate	KsKfA	Exhort	KsRd
Excavation	KsKfAShn	Exhortation	KsRShn
Excel	KsL	Exigency	KsJNS
Excellency	KsNS	Exile	KSl
Excellent	KsNd	Exist-ence	KSst
Exceptionable	KsPsNB	Existent	KSsN
Excess	KSs	Exonerate	KsNRT
Excessive	KSsV	Exorbitant	KsRB
Exchange	KsCh	Exorcise	KsRSs
Exchequer	KsChK	Exordium	KsRDm
Excite	KsT	Expect-ation	KsPK
Excitement	KsTcM	Expectancy	KsPKNS
Exclaim-ation	SKlm	Expectorate-ion	KsPKR
Exclamatory	SKlmTR	Expediency	KsPtNS
Exclude	SKl	Expedient	KsPtN
Exclusion	SKlshn	Expedite	KsPtT
Exclusive	SKls$V$	Expedition	KsPtshn
Excommunicate-ion	Ks-YnK	Expeditious	KsPShs
Excruciating	KsKRSh	Expel	KsPl
Exculpate	KsKlP	Expenditure	KsPnCh

Experience	K¹sP	**F**	
Experiment	KsPM	Facetious	FSShs
Expert	KsP*R*d	Facility-ate	F¹S
Expiate-ion	KsP:*E*A	Fact	F³
Expire-ation	K¹sP*R*	Faculty	*F*KT
*Explain-ation	SPln	Fade	*F*D
Explicit	SPlsT	Familiar-ity	F¹M
Explode	SPlt	Familiarize	FMs
Explore-ation	SPl*R*	Familiarization	F¹MsShn
Export-ation	KsP*R*	Family	F³M
Expostulate	KsPsChlT	Fanaticism	*F*nTsM
*Express	S*P*s	Fancy	FnS
*Expressage	S*P*sZh	Fantastic	FntSt
*Extemporaneous	KsTmP	Farm	F*R*M
*Extempore	KsTmP*R*	Farther	Frtr
*Extemporary	KsTmRR	Fashionable	FsNBl
*Extension	KsTshn	Fatal	FT*l*
Extenuate	KsTnT	Father	FDh
*Extenuation	KsTnshn	Favor	Ff
Exterminate-ion	KsRMN	Favorable	FB
External	KsRNl	Favored	Fft
*Extinct-ion	KsNg	Favorite	FfRt
*Extinguish	KsNgSh	Favoritism	FfRsM
Extra	KstR	Felicity	FlStE
*Extract	K³sT	Fellow	Fl³
Extraction	K³sTshn	Felonious	FloNs
Extraordinary	KsRd	Ferocious	*F*RShs
Extravagance	KsTfGns	Fervent	FrVnt
Extravasation	KsTfASshn	Festive-ity	F¹³sTf
Extreme	KsRM	Fever	FfR
*Extricate	KstK	Fidelity	*F*DT
*Exuberance-t	KsB:u	Filial	F*ll*
*Exude	KsD:u	Final	FNl
Eye	I¹	Finance	*F*NNs
Eyeball	IB*l*	Finely	FNl
Eyebrow	IBr	Finite	*F*nT
Eyelash	ILSh	First	Fst

Flight	*F*1T	*Gamble-r	GmB
*Fluent	Flnt	*Gambol	GmB*l*
Food	*F*D	*Game	GM
*Fool	F*l*	*Garden	GrDn
Footstep	Fst*P*	Gather	Gtr
Foreign-er	*F*rN	General	Jn
*Forenoon	*F*rNN	Generality	JnTi
Foreordination	Fr*R*Nshn	Generalization	Jsshn
Forest	*F*Rst	Generalize	Jns
Forever	FV	Generation	Jshn
*Form	Fr¹	*Genesis	JNsS
Formal-ly-ity	Fr*l*	Genial	JN*l*(u)
Formation	Frshn	*Genius	JNs
Former-ly	Fr*R*	*Genteel	J¹nT*l*
Forth	FTh	*Gentile	J²nT*l*
Fortunate	*F*rChnT	*Gentle	Jnt*l*
*Forward	*F*rR	Gentleman	Jnt³
Freedom	*F*rDm	Gentlemen	Jnt²
Freight	Frt	Genuflection	Jn*F*Kshn
Frequency	FrnS	Genuine	JnN
Frequent	Frnt	*Genus	JNs:eu
From	"from"	Geometry	JMTr
*Froward	Fr*w*R	*Go	G³
*Fruition	FrShn	*God	G¹
Fulfill	Fl³F	Good	G⁸
*Funeral	FnR*l*	Govern-ment	Gf
*Funereal	FN*Rl*	Governor	G*fR*
Furnish	Frn	Gracious	GrAShs
Furniture	*F*rnChR	Graduate	GrcJT
Futility	*F*TT	Gradual	GrJl
Future	*F*ChR	Graphic	Grf*E*K
Futurity	.*F*ChT	Gravitation	GrTshn
		Gravity	GrT
G		*Gray	GrA
Galaxy	G1KS	*Great	Gr
Gallant	G*l*N	Guarantee	GrnTi
Galvanize	Gl*f*Ns	*Guardian	GRdN

140 LIGHT—LINE SHORTHAND.

*Guide	GD	Heterogeneous	HRJNs
Gymnasium	JmNsM	Hieroglyphic	HRGlK
Gymnast	JmNst	Him	H¹
Gymnastics	JmNst*is*	Himself	Hs¹
		His	s¹

H

		History	HsR
Habeas Corpus	HBsK	Hitherto	HDhr "to"
Habit	HB	Homeopathy-ic	Hm*P*Th
Habitation	HBshn	Homogeneous	HmJNs
Habitual	HBChl	Horizon-tal	HRsN
Hair	Hr	Horse	Hrs
Halleluiah	H*lL*	Horticulture-al	HrK*l*
Hamlet	HMlt	Horticulturist	HrK*l*st
Hamper	Hm*P*R	Hostility	HsTT
Handkerchief	HnChf	Hottentot	HTnTT
Handsome	HnsM	Housewife	HsWf
Harbor	HrB	However	H³v
Harmonic	*R*mN*i*K	Human	HmN
Harmonica	*R*mN*A*	Humanity	HmNT
Harmonious	*R*mNs	Humbug	HBG
Harmony	*R*mN	Humility	HMlT
Hazy	HAZ	Hundred	Hnt
Health	H*l*Th	*Hypercritical	HPKrTKl
Heaven	HN	*Hypocrite-ical	HPKT
Help	H*l*P	Hypothecate	H*P*Th
Hemisphere	HmSF	Hysterics	Hs*R*Ks
Henceforth	HsFTh		
Her	Hr		
Here	Hr¹		I
Hereafter	Hr¹F	I	I¹
Hereditament	HrdM	Iambic	IMBK
Hereditary	HrR	Ibex	*I*BKs
*Herein	Hrn	*Ice	IS
*Hereon	HrN	Idea	*I*D
Heretofore	Hr*F*r	Ideal-ly	*I*D*L*
Herewith	Hr*w*(l)	Ideality	*I*DT
Heterodox	HdoDs	Identify	*I*DnF
		Idiocy	*E*DS

Idiom	*E*DcM	*Impudent	MPtNd
Idiosyncrasy	DsNKrS	*Impure-ity	MP*R*
Idiot	*E*Dt	Inaccessible-ility	nKSs*B*
Idle	IDl	Inadvertent-ly	nD *V*rTnt
Idol	I D*l*	Inalienable	N*L*NBl
Idolater	*I*D*l*R	Inauguration	NGrshn
*Idolatry	D*l*R	Incapable	nKPB
Illustrate-ion-rious	*L*(b)sT	*Incessant	NsSnt
Imaginary	Jn³R	Incipient	NsPNt
Imagination	J³shn	Incognito	N¹-NT
Imagine	Jn³	Incoherent	nKHrN
Immaterial	EM³T	Inconsiderable	NsDB
Immature	EMTR	Inconsiderate	NsDRd
Immeasurable	EMZh	*Inconsistent	NSsNt
Immediate-ly	M¹D	Incontrovertible	nKnt*V*rB
Immemorial	EMMR*l*	Inconvenience-t	N*V*n
Immigrant	EMGrnt	Incredible-ility	NKrDB
Immigrate	EMGrT	Incredulity	NKrJlT
Immoral-ity	iMr*l*	Indeed	nDt
Immortal-ity	iMrd	Indefatigable	Nt*F*GB
Immovable	EMvABl	Indemnify	nDmN*F*
Impalpable	MPP*B*	Indemnity	nDmNT
Impartial	MPSh	Independence-t	nDPnt
*Impassionate	MPshnT	Indescribable	nDsKB*B*
*Impassioned	M³Pshnt	Indestructible	nDstR*B*
Impatience	MPshns	Indeterminable	nDtMB
Impenetrable-ility	MPnTB	*Indeterminate	nDtMN
Imperceptible	MPsP*B*	Index	NtKs
*Imponderable	MPntB	Indicate	NtK
Import	MP*R*	Indication	Nt¹Kshn
Importance-t	M¹P	Indict-ment	nDt
Importation	MP*R*Tshn	Indifferent	nD¹
*Improbable-ility	MP*B*	*Indignant	NtGnt
Impromptu	MPmPtu	Indignation	NtGshn
*Improper-priety	M¹PP	Indignity	NtGnT
Improve-ment	M³Pf	Indirect	NDrK
*Imprudent	MPuNd	Indiscriminate-ion	nDsKM

Indispensable	nDsPns	*Ingenuous-ness	nJNS
Individual	nDfJ	Inhabit-ant	NIIB
Indoctrinate	NDrnT:A	Inherent	NHrnt
Indolent	Nt*L*N	Inherit	NH*r*T
Indomitable	nDcMTB	*Iniquity	nKT
Indorse	NDrs	Injure-y	NJr
Indulge	NtJ	Injurious	NJrs
*Indulgence	NtJns	Ink	NgK
*Indulgent	NtJnt	*Innovation	NoVshn
Industry	nDstR	*Innoxious	NnKShs
Indwelling	NDl-*e*	Innuendo	NYnD
Ineffectual	N*F*KChl	Innutrition	*E*NTrshn
Inefficient	nFShnt	Inodorous	NoDRs
Inequitable	NKlTB	Inordinate	N*R*DnT
Inertia	NrSh	Inquire-y	NWr
*Inevitable	N*V*TB	Inquisition	NKlsshn
Inexhaustible	nKSst*B*	Inquisitive	NKlsTf
Inexperience	nKsP	Insecure	NsK
Inexplicable	NSPlKB	Insecurity	NsKT
Inexpressible	*N*¹S*P*s*B*	*Insert	Ns*R*T
*Infallible-ility	N*F*lB	Insinuate	NsNY
Infant	N*F*nt	Insolent	NSlnt
Infer-ence	N⁹*F*	Insolvency	NSlfNS
Inferior-ity	N*F*RR	Inspect-ion	NsPK
Infidel	N*F*D	Inspire-ation	N¹sP*R*
Infidelity	N*F*DT	Install-ation	N¹sT*l*
Infinite-y	N*F*nT	Instruct-ion	NsK
Infinitude	N*F*nTt	*Instrument	N¹st
Infirm	N*F*rM	Insubordinate-ion	NsBtN
Inflect	N*F*K	Insufficient	NSFSh
Influence	N¹s	Insult	NSlt
Influential	N¹Sh	Insurance	NsYs
Informal-ity	NFr*l*	Insure	NsY
Information	Nshn¹	*Integrity	nTGrT
Infrequent	NFrnt	Intellect	NtK
*Ingenious	nJNs	Intellectual	Nt¹KChl
Ingenuity	nJNT	*Intelligence-t	NtJ

LIGHT—LINE SHORTHAND. 143

Intemperance	nTmPns		Iron		RN
Intemperate	nTmP		Irresistible		ERsS
Intend-t	NtNd		Issue		ESh
Interchange	Nt¹Ch		It		T²
Intercourse	NtKRs		Italian		TLN
*Interest-ed	Ntst		Italic		TLK
*Interesting	Ntst-e		*Item		ITm
Interfere	NtF		Itself		T²s
*Interior	nT¹RR				
Intermediate	NtMD		**J**		
Interminable	NtMnB		Jealous		Jls
Intermingle	NtMNgl		Journal		JRNl
Internal	NTrn		Judge		J²
*International	NtNsNl		*Judicial		JDSh
*Interpret	NPt		*Judicious		JDShs
*Interpretation	NPshn		Jurisdiction		JrsDshn
Interrogate-ion	NRG		Jurisprudence		JrsPtNs
*Interrupt	nTPt		Juror		JRR
Intersect	NTrsK		Jury		JR
Intertwine	NTrTn		Justify		JsF
Interval	NtVl		Juvenile		Jf²
Intimate	NtM		Juxtaposition		JKsPsshn
Intimidate	nTmDt				
Into	nT¹		**K**		
Intolerant	nTLRN		Kingdom		K¹
Intoxicate-ion	NtKsK		Knew		N²
Intractable	NTrTB		Know		"Know"
Inure	NY		Knowledge		nJ¹
Invalid	NVlD				
Invention	NVnshn		**L**		
Investigate-ion	NVsG		Label		LBl
Inviolable	NVlB		Labor		LBr
Inviolate	NVlT		Lacerate		LsRt
Invulnerable	NVlnRB		*Lad		Ld
Inward	NwR		*Lady		lD
Iodine	IoDn		Lamp		lMP
Irish	IRSh		Land		Lnt

Landscape	LnSKP	Lightning	LtNg
Language	Ng³	Lily	LL
Lantern	Lnt*R*N	*Limit	LM
Lard-oil	LRt*L*	Linger	LNg
Large	J³	Lion	L*I*N
Largely	Jl³	Liquid	LKlD
Larger	Jr³	Literary	LtRR
Larynx	LRNgs	*Literature	LRCh
*Last	*l*(d)st²	Little	L¹
*Latitude	LtTt	Live	V¹
Laughter	*lF*tr	Long	Ng¹
Laureate	L*R*T	Lord	*R*d¹
Lavish	*lVE*s	Love	V²
Law	L¹(f)	Low	Lo
Lawsuit	"Law" St	Loyal-ty	L*l*
Lawyer	"Law" *R*	Ludicrous	LtKs
Leather	LD*h*	Lumber	LMr
*Lecture	LC*h*r	Luxuriant	*l*(d)KsRnt
Left	*l*(u)*F*		
Legal	LGl	**M**	
Legerdemain	LJDmN	Made	Md
*Legislate-ure	LJ	Magic	McJK
*Legislation	LJshn	Magistrate	McJsRd
*Legislator	LJR	Magnificent	M¹sNd
Leisure	LZ*h*	Mainland	MNlNt
Lenient	*l*NNd	Majority	McJT
Let	*l*²(u)	Make	M²
Letter	LR	Maker	MKr
Liable	LBl	Malevolent	MlVlnt
Liberal-ity	Br¹*L*	Malicious	MlShs
Liberate	LBrt	Malignant-ity	MlG
Libertine	LBrtN	Manifesto	MnFsto
Liberty	Br¹	Manly	MNl
Lieutenant	LtNNd	Manner	mNr
Life	F¹	Maneuver	MNVr
Lifeless	F¹Ls	Manslaughter	MsLR
Lifetime	F¹;M	Manual	MNl

*Manufactory	MnFtR	Metaphor-ical	M²TFr
*Manufacture	MnF	Metaphysical	MtFsK
*Manufacturer	MnFR	Method-ical	M²cTht
Manuscript	MsKP	Methodism	McThsM
*Mar	MR	Methodist	McThst
March	MRCh	Metropolis	MPLs
*Mark	Mr	Metropolitan	MPLTn
Market	MrT	Midnight	MDnT
Marsh	MrSh	Midst	Mtst
Marvelous	MrVls	Might	MT
Masculine	MsKlN	Military	MlR
Master	MsR	Milk	MlK
*Material	M³T	Millennium	MlnM
Materiality	MTLT	Million	Ml¹
Mathematics	McThMs	Mineral	MnRl
Matrimony	MdMN	Miniature	MnChR
*Matter	M³	*Minister	MnS
*Mature	MTR	*Ministerial	MnSl
Maturity	MTT	*Ministration	MnSshn
Meander	MNtr	*Ministry	MnSR
Measure	MZh	Minstrel	MsRl
*Medial	MDl	Miracle	MrKl
Medium	Md¹M	Misapply	M³sP:I
Melancholy	MlnK	Misapprehension	M³sPnshn
Member	MM	Misdemeanor	MsMnR
Memoranda	MMnD	Misfortune	MsF
Memorandum	MMnDm	Misrepresent-ation	MsRP
Mention	MnShn	Missionary	MsNR
Merchandise	MrDs	*Mistake	MsT
Merchant	MrcChnt	Mistaken	MsTn
Merciful	MRSf	*Mistook	M³sT
*Mercury	MrKri	Mistrust	MsTst
Mercy	MRS	Misunderstand-ing	MsNsTnt
Messenger	MsNJr	Mitigate	MtG
Metal-lic	M¹tl(ub)	Moderate	MDrt
Metallurgy	MtlJ	Modern	MDrn
Metamorphosis	MMRFss	Modernize	MDrnls

Modest	Mtst	Myth	McTh
Modification	MdFshn	Mythology-ical	MThlJ
Modify	MdF		
Modulate	MJlT	**N**	
Mohammedan	MMDn	Naked	nKD
Money	mN	Name	Nm
Monitor	MnTR	Narrate	NRT
Monopoly	MnPL	Narrow	NR
*Monster	Mst$R$	Nation-al	Nshn
Monstrosity	Mst$R$sT	Nationality	NsNlT
Month	MnTh	Native-ity	nTf²
Moonlight	MNlt	Nature-al	NChr
Moral-ity	Mr¹l	Navigate-ion	NfG
More	Mr	Navy·al	NV
Morning	Mrn	*Nearest	Nrst
Mortal-ity	Mrd¹	Near-ly	Nr
*Mortgage	MRG	Necessary-ily	NsR
*Mortgagee	MRJ	Necessity	NsT
*Mortgagor	MRJR	Neglect	NGlK
Mortification	MrdFshn	Negligence	NGlns
Mother	McDh	Negligent	NGlnt
Mourn	Mrn	*Negro	NGr
Mouth	McTh	Nerve	Nrv
Much	Ch³	Nervous	Nrvs
Multifarious	Mlt$F$Rs	Neuralgia	NRlJ
Multiform	Mlt$F$	Never	N¹
Multiply	MlP	Nevertheless	N¹l(r)s
Multitude	MlTt	New	N³
Municipal	MnSP	Newspaper	NsPPr
Municipality	MnSPT	Next	Nst
Munificent	MnFSnt	*Nigger	nGR
Murder	Mrtr	No	"no"
Murderer	MrtrR	Nobody	"no" Bt
Mutilate-ion	M³uL	Nomenclature	NKlChr
Mutual	MChl	*Nominate-ion	N¹mN
*Mystery	MstR	*Nominee	NmNi
Mystify	Ms TF	None	"no" n(f)

Nonconformity	NN-FrMT	**O**	
Nondescript	NNsKP	Oar	or
Nonsuit	NNSt	Oasis	oAS²s
*Noon	NN	Oats	ots
Nor	Nr	Obdurate	awBtRd
Normal	NrMl	Obedient	oBtNd
North	NrTh	*Obey	oB
*Northeast	NrSt	Object	J¹
Northeastern	NrSn	Objection	Jshn¹
Northward	Nr*w*R	Objectionable	JsNBl
Northwest	Nr*w*st	Objective	J¹Tf
Nostril	Nst*Kl*	Objector	J¹eu
Nostrum	Nst*R*M	Obligation	BG
Not	Nt	Oblige	BJ
Notary	nTR	Obliterate-ion	B*L*R
Note	Nt	Oblivion	BlfN
Nothing	I²Th †	Obscure	BsKR
Notice	nTs	Obscurity	BsKT
Notify	NtF	Obsequious	BsKWs
Notification	NtFshn	Observe-ance	BsR
Notoriety	nTR*I*T	Observatory	BsRdR
Notwithstanding	N¹sTnt	*Obsolete	BSlt
Nourish-ment	NrSh	Obstacle	BsK*l*
*Novelty	NVlE	*Obstruct-ion	BsK
November	NfM	Obtain	BtN
Novitiate	nVSht	Occasion-al	Kshn
Now	N³	*Occupy	KuP
Number	NMr	Octavo	KTfo
Numeration	NMrshn	Ocular	Ku*L*R
Numerator	NMreu	Odd	awd
Nun	NN	Odious	oDs
Nunnery	NN*R*	Odor	oDR
Nuptials	NPShs	Of	"of"
Nurse	Nrs	Offence	*F*ns
Nurture	NrChr	Offend	*F*nt
Nymph	NmF	Offensive	Fs*V*

† "no" is struck in the direction of R.

Offer	Fr	Ordinance	RNNs
Official	FSh	Ordinary	Rd^1
Officious	FShs	Ordination	RNshn
Offspring	FPrNg	Ordnance	RNNs
Often	Fn	Ore	or
Oil	awi	Organ	RGn
Ointment	NtMnt	Organic	R^1GnK
Old	ol	Organism	RGnsM
Olio	oL^2	Organize-ation	R^1GNs
Omnipotent	MnPtNd	Orient-al	RNt
Omnipresent	MnPsNd	Origin	RJn
On	"on"	Original-ity-ate	R^1J
Once	wNs	Ornament-al	R^1nM
One	wN	Ornamentation	RnMnShn
Only	Nl	Ornithology	RNThlJ
Onward	"on" wR	Orphan	RFn
Opaque	oPK	Orphanage	RFnZh
*Open	oPn	Orthodox-y	R^1Th
Opera	awPR	Ostentation	StNShn
Operate	P^1R	Ostentatious	StNShs
Operator	P^1Rtr	Ostracise	STrsIs
Opiate	oPt	Ostracism	STrsM
Opinion	PnN	Other	"other"
Opportune	PTn	Ought	T^1
Opportunity	PTnT	Our	R^3
Opposition	awPsshn	Ourselves	Rss^3
*Oppress	Prs^1	Out	T^3
*Oppression	Prshn^1	Outer	T^{3}R
*Oppressive	Prs^{1}V	Outlaw	T^3L
Optician	PtiShn	Outlawry	T^3LR
Orang-outang	RNgNg	Outline	T^3lN
*Orator	RdR	Outlive	T^3Lv
*Oratory	RdRi	Outrage	T^{3}RJ
*Oratorio	RTR	Outset	T^{3}sT
Ordain	RN	Outside	T^{3}sD
Order-ly	RR	Outspread	T^{3}sPt:e
Ordinal	RNl	Outstretch	T^{3}stRCh

LIGHT-LINE SHORTHAND. 149

Outstrip	T³stRP	Owl	ow²l
Outvote	T³cVt	Own	N³
Outwalk	T³cwK	Owner	Nr
Outward	T³wR	Oyster	Str
Outwear	T³wR		
Outwit	T³wiT	**P**	
Outwork	T³wRK	Pacific	PsFK
Oval	oVl³	Painter	Pntr
Ovary	oVR	Pair	PR
Oven	euVn	Pamphlet	PmFT
Over	Vr³	Panacea	PNSA
Overawe	Vr²aw	Panel	PNl
Overbalance	Vr²Blns	Panther	PnThR
Overbear-ing	Vr³BR	Pantomime	PnMM
Overboard	VrBRd	Paper	PPr
Overcharge	Vr²Ch	Parade	PRD
Overcome	VrK	Parallel	PrL
Overdo	Vr²D	Paralysis	PrLsS
Overhear	Vr³HR	Paralytic	PrLK
Overland	VrlN	Paralyze	PrLs
Overlook	Vr²lK	Paraphernalia	PrFNL
Overpower	Vr³Pr	Parasite	PRsT
Overrate	VrRT	*Parasol	Prs$L$
Overrule	Vr²Rl	*Parcel	Prs$l$
Overrun	VrRN	Parchment	PrChM
Oversight	VrSt	Pardon	PRDn
*Oversleep	Vr²slP	Parent-al	P³nT
Overspread	Vrs$P$D	Parentage	PnTcJ
*Overstep	Vrst$P$	Parenthesis	PrnThsS
Overt	oVrT	Parish	PrSh
Overtake	VrT	Park	PRK
Overture	VrChR	Parliament-ary	P³L
Overturn	VrTn	Parole	PRl
Overwhelm-ing	VrlM	Paroxysm	PRKsM
Overwork	VrwR	Parsimonious	PrsMNs
Owe	o	Parson	PRsN
Owing	o-e	Parsonage	PRsJ

Part	P³	Pedigree	PtGi
Partial	PrSh	Peevish	PVSh
Partiality	PrShT	Pegasus	PGASs
Participate-ion	P¹RTsP	Pelf	PlF
Particle	PRTKl	Penalty	PNlT
Particular	P¹rtK	Pencil	PNsl(u)
Partisan	PtsN	Pendency	PnNS
Part-owner	PtNR	Pendulous	PnJls
Partner	PrNr	Pendulum	PnJM
Party	P³	Penetrate	PnTt
Passenger	PsNJr	Penetration	PnTshn
Passionate	PshnT	Peninsular	PnNShL
Pastime	PsM	Penitential	PnTSh
Pasture	PsChr	Penitentiary	PnTShR
Patent	PtNd	Penny	PN
Patentee	PtNdE	*People	P³P
Paternal	PtRNl	Perfect-ion	PfK
Paternity	PtRnti	Perform-ance	PrFr
Pathetic	PTht	Perfume	PrfM
Pathology	PThlJ	Perhaps	H³Ps
Patience	Pshns	Peril	PrL
Patient	Pshnt	Period	PRD
Patriarch	PtRRK	Perish	PrSh
Patrician	PtRshn	Perjury	PrJr
Patriot-ic	PtRd	Permanent	PrmNNd
Patriotism	PtRsM	Permit-ssion	PrM
Patrol	PtRl	Peroration	PRRshn
*Patron	PTrn	Perpendicular	PrPnD
Patronage	PtJ	Perpetual	PrPChl
Patronize	PTrnIs	Perplexity	PrPKsT
*Pattern	PtRn	Perquisite	PrKsT
Pavilion	PVln	*Persecute-ion	Ps³K
Pawnbroker	PnBKR	Persevere	PrsVR
Peculiar-ity	PKl	Persist	PrZst
Pecuniary	PKnR	Person	PrsN
Pedantic	PtNtK	Personification	PrsNFshn
Pedestrian	PtAsRN	Perspective	PrsPKTf

Persuade	PrSlt	Pitiable	Pti*B*
Pertain	PrtN	Pitiful	PtF
Pertinacious	PrtNShs	Pity	Pti
Pertinent	PrtNNd	Plagiarism	PlJrsM
Perturbation	PrtR*B*shn	Plainly	PlNl
Perusal	P*R*sl	Planet	PlnT
Pervade	PrfD	Platform	Plt*F*r
Pervert	Pr*V*rT	Platonic	PltNcK
Perversity	Pr*V*rsT	Platoon	PltuN
Pestilence	Ps*l*Ns	Pleasure	Zh²
Petard	PtaRd	Plenipotentiary	PlnPtNSh
Petition	Ptshn	Pliant	PlNd
Petrify	PtF	*Plodder	PltR
Petroleum	PtRM	*Plotter	Pltr
Pettish	PtiSh	Plumage	PlmJ
Petty	Pti	Plunderer	PlntrR
Petulant	PChlnt	Pneumatics	N-Ms
Phantasm	FntZm	Poet	PT
Pharisee	FrS	Poetical	PTKl
Phenomenon	FnMNN	Poetry	PTr
Philanthropy-ic	Fln³Th*P*	Polar	P*L*R
Philosopher	Fls*FR*	Polarization	P*L*RsShn
Philosophy-ical	FlsF	Pole-star	P*l*(u)st*R*
*Physical	*F*sK	Police	Plis
Physician	FZshn	Police Officer	Pls*F*s*R*
Piano	PN	Policy	PlS
Picture	PKChr	Polish	PlSh
Piety	P*I*T	Polite-ness	P*L*
Pilgrim	PlGrm	*Politic	P*L*K
Pilotage	P*L*dZh	*Political	PlK
Pimple	PmP*l*	Politician	Pltshn
Pious	PS	Politics	PlKs
Piquancy	PKNS	Poll-tax	P*l*(d)Ks
Piquant	PKNd	Polygamy	P*L*G
Piracy	PRS	Polygamist	P*L*Gst
Pistol	Pst*l*	Pony	PoN
Piteous	Ptis	*Poor	P*R*

Pope	PP	Pre-existence	PrKSst
Popular-ity	P¹P*LR*	*Prefer-ence	Pr*F*
Populate-ation	P¹P*L*	Pregnant	PrGNN
Portable	P*R*TB	Prejudice	PrJDs
Portfolio	P*R*dF*l*	Prejudicial	PrJDSh
Portion	Prshn	Premeditated	PrMD
Portray	PrTr	Premier	PrMr
Position	Psshn	*Premise	PrmIs
*Possess-ion	*Ps*S	*Premises	PrmASs
Possessive	*Ps*Sf	Premium	PrMM
Possessor	*Ps*S*R*	Prepare-ation	Pr³P*R*
Possible-ility	PsB	Preponderate-ion	PrPnt
Postage	PsJ	Preponderance	Pr¹PnNs
Posterity	PsTT	Prepossessing	Pr*Ps*S
Postmaster	PsMs*R*	Prerogative	Pr*R*G
Post-office	Ps*F*s	Presbyterian	PrsB*R*N
Posture	PsChr	Presentation	PrsNShn
Potentate	PtNTt	Preserve-ation	PrsR
Potential	PtNSh	Presidency	PrsDS
Poverty	PfT	Presidential	PrsDSh
Powder	Ptr	Presumptuous	PrsMPChs
*Power	Pr³	*Pretend	PrtNd
Powerful	Prf	Preternatural	PrtrNChr
*Practicable	PrKB	Pretext	PrtKst
Practice-al	PrK	Pretty	Prti
Precede	PrsD	Prevail-lence-t	PrVl
Precinct	PrsNg	Prevaricate-ion	Pr³*V*rK
Precipitate	PrsPtT	Prevent	PrfNd
Precise	PrSs	Previous-ly	Pr*V*s
Preclude	PrKl	Price-list	Prs*l*st
Preconcerted	Pr-Srt*t*	Priestcraft	PrsKft
Predecessor	PrtiSs*R*	Primary	PrMr
Predicate	PrtKT	Primitive	PrMTf
Predict	PrtK	Primogeniture	PrmJnChR
Predominate	PrtMN	*Principal-le	PrsP
*Pre-eminent	PrMNN	Prisoner	PrsN*R*
Pre-engagement	PrnGM	*Private	PrfT

LIGHT-LINE SHORTHAND. 153

Privation	PrfAShn	*Promise	PrMs
Privilege	PrfJ	*Promote	PrmT
*Probable-ility	Pr*B*	Promotion	PrmsN
Probation	PrBshn	Prompt	PrmPt
Probationer	PrBsN*R*	Promulgate-ion	PrMlG
Probity	PrBti	Pronounce	PrnNs
Problem	PrBm	Pronunciation	PrnNShshn
Problematical	PrB-M	Propel	PrP*l*(u)
Procedure	PrsJr	Proper	PrP
Proceed	PrsD	Property	PrP
Process	PrSs	Prophecy-sy	PrFS
Procession	PrSshn	*Prophet	PrFt
Proclivity	PrKlf*ET*	Prophetess	PrFtAs
Procrastinate	PrKrstN	Proportion-al	PrPshn
Procure	PrKR	Proportionable	PrPsN*B*
Prodigal	Prt*G*	Proportionate	PrPshnT
Prodigious	PrtJs	Proprietor	PrPtr
*Produce	Prtus	Propriety	PrP
Product	PrtK	Propulsion	PrP*l*(u)Shn
Production	PrtKshn	Prorogation	Pr*R*Gshn
Profanation	Pr*F*nAShn	Prorogue	Pr*R*G
Profane	Pr*F*n	*Prosecute	PrsKT
Profession-al	Pr*F*shn	Prosecution	PrsKshn
Professor	Pr*F*sR	Prospect	PrsPK
Proficiency	PrFShnS	Prosperity	PrsP*R*T
Proficient	PrFSh	Prostitute	PrsTTt
*Profit	PrfT	Prostrate	PrsTt
Profligacy-te	Prf*l*G	*Protect-ion	PrtK
Profound	Pr*F*nt	*Protest	PrTst
Profusion	Pr*F*shn	Protestant	PrsTnt
Prognostic-ate	PrGNst	Protestantism	PrsTsM
Prognostication	PrGNstShn	Protestation	PrTsTshn
Prognosticator	PrGNst*R*	Protract	PrTr
Prohibit-ion	PrHB	Protraction	PrTrshn
Prolong-ation	Pr*l*(u)Ng	Protuberance	PrtuBns
Promenade	PrMNd	Proverb-ial	Prf'R*B*
Prominent	PrmNNd	Provide	PrfD

154 LIGHT-LINE SHORTHAND.

Providential	PrfDSh	Putrescent	PtRsNt
Provincial	PrfNSh	Putrid	PtD
Provision-al	Pr*V*shn	Pyramid	P*R*M
Provocation	Pr*V*Kshn	Pyriform	P*R*Fr
*Provoke	Pr*V*K	Pyrotechnics	P*R*TnKs
Proximate-ity	PrKsMT		
Prudent	PrtNd	**Q**	
Prudish	PrtiSh		
*Public-ish	PB	*Quack	K*w*K
*Publication	PBshn	Quadrangle-ular	K¹DRNg
*Publisher	PBSh	Quadrant	KDRnt
Puerile	Pu*R*l	Quadratic	KDRK
Pugilist	PJlst	Quadrennial	KDRNl
Pulpit	PlP	Quadrille	KDR*l*
Pulsation	Pl(u)sShn	Quadrumanous	KDRmNs
Pulverization	Pl*V*rsshn	Quadruped	KDPt
Punctual	PnCh*l*	Quaff	K*w*F
Punctuation	PnChshn	Quail	Kl*l*
*Punish-ment	PNSh	Quaint	K*w*Nd
*Pure	Pr³	Quaker	KKR
Purgatory	P*R*GR	Qualification	KlFshn
*Purification	PrFshn	Qualify	KlF
*Purify	PrF	Quality	KlT
Puritan	PrTn	Quandary	KlntR
Puritanism	PrTnsM	Quantity	KntT
Purity	PrT	Quarantine	KlRuN
Purple	PrP*l*	Quarrel	KR*l*
Purport	PrP*R*T	Quarry	K*w*R
Purpose-ly	PPs	Quart	KlRd
Pursuance	PrSns	Quarter-ly	KRR
Pursuant	PrSut	Quartette	KRtT
Pursue	PrS	Quash	K*w*(r)Sh
Purulence-t	Pru*L*	Quasi	KAZ
Pusillanimous	Ps*l*NMs	Queen	Kln
Put	P³	Queer	KR
*Putrefaction	PtR*F*shn	Quench	KlnCh
*Putrefy	PtR*F*	Quest	Kst:*w*
		Question	KsChn

Quibble	KB*l*	*Reaction	*R*aKshn
Quick	KK	*Read	Rd
Quicksilver	KSlVr	*Reader	RdR
Quiescent	KWsNt	Ready	*R*D
Quiet	KT	Real-ity	R¹*l*
Quill	Kl*l*	Realize	R*l*s
Quinine	KNN	Realization	R*l*sShn
Quinsy	KlNZ	Reason	RsN
Quire	KR	Rebel	RBl
Quit	KT	Rebellion	RYn
Quit-claim	KTKlM	Recall	RKl
Quiver	Kl*V*r	Recapitulate	*R*KPChT
Quiz	K*w*s	Recede	RSt
Quorum	KRM	Receipt	RSt
Quoth	KcTh	*Receive	RSf
Quotient	Kshnt:*w*	Recent	RsNt
		*Recess	RSs
R		Reciprocal	RsPK*l*
Race-horse	RsHRs	*Reciprocate	RsPKT
*Rack	*R*aK	Reciprocity	RSPrsT
Radiant	*R*Dnt	*Recite	RsT
Radical	*R*DKl	Reclaim	RKlM
Rafter	R*F*tr	Recognize	RNs
Railroad	R*R*	Recognizance	RNsNs
Railway	*R*W	Recoil	*R*K*l*
Ramify	RmF	Recollect	R³
Rancid	RnSt	Recollection	Rshn³
Rapacious	*R*PShs	Recommence	R-Ns
Rapacity	*R*PsT	*Recommit	R-T
Rapid	*R*Pt	*Reconcile	R-S
Rapidity	*R*PtT	*Reconciliation	R-Sshn
Rapture	*R*PChr	*Reconsideration	RsDshn
Ration-al	Rshn	*Reconstruct-ion	R²sK
Rationality	Rshnt*i*	Record	R¹Kr
Ravish	RVSh	Recorder	RKrR
Reach	RCh	Recourse	RKrs
*React	*R*aK	Recover-able	*R*Kf

Recreation	RKrshn	Regulation	RGshn
Recriminate-ion	RKrmN	Rehearse	RHRs
Rectangle	RKNg	Reiterate-ion	RTR
Rectify	RKF	Reject	RJK
Rectitude	RKTt	Relate-ive	Rl
Recur	RKr	Relation	RShn
Recurrent	RKrnt	Relax	RlKs
Redeem	RDm	Relevant	RlVnt
Redemption	RDmshn	Relevancy	RlVn
Redolent	RDlnt	Relief	RlF
Reduce	RDs	Relieve	RlV
Reduction	RDshn	Religion	Jn¹
Redundance	RtNNs	Religious	Js¹
Reduplication	RDPKshn	Relinquish-ment	RlNg
Re-election	RLKshn	Reluctance-t	RlK
Re-enforce	RnFRs	*Remark	RMr
*Refer-ence	RF	Remarkable	RMrB
Referee	RFR	Remedy	RMD
*Reflect-ion	RFK	Remember	RMM
*Reform	RFr	Remembrance	RMMs
Reformation	RFrshn	Remit-tance	R¹M
Reformer	RFrR	Remonstrance	RMsTns
*Refract	RFrK	Remonstrate	RMsTt
*Refraction	RFrKshn	Remorse	RMrs
Refrigerate-ion	RFrJ	Remunerate-ion	RMnR
Refuge	RFJ	Render	RntR
Refugee	RFJi	Rendition	RntShn
Refute-ation	RFT	Renew	RN
Regal	RGl	Renunciation	RnNShshn
Regale	RGl	Reorganize-ation	RRGNs
Regalia	RGla	*Repair	RPr
*Regard	R³	Repeal	RPl
Regardful	RGrtF	Repeatedly	RPtL
Register	RJsR	*Repel	RPl
Registration	RJsRshn	Repent-ance	RPnt
*Regret	RGr	Repetition	RPTshn
Regular-ity-ate	R²G	Replenish	RPlNSh

Replevin	RPlfN	Resolve	RsV
Report	RPrt	Resort	Rs*R*T
Reporter	RPrtr	*Resources	RsSs
Reprehend	RPrnD	Respect-ful-ly	RsPK
Reprehensible	RPrnsB	Respective	RsPKf
Reprehension	RPrnshn	Resplendency	RsPnNS
Reprehensive	RPrns *V*	Respond-ent	RsPnt
Represent-ation	R*P*	Response-ible-ibility	RsPns
Representative	R*P*f	Restaurant	RsTrnt
Reproduce	RPrtus	Restore	Rst*R*
Republic	R*P*B	Restrain	RsTrn
Republican	R*P*Bn	Restrict	Rs*R*K
Republish	R*P*B	Result	Rs*l*
Republication	R*P*Bshn	Resuscitate-ion	RsS*i*T
Repugnance-t	R*P*G	Retail	Rt*L*
Repulsion	R*Pu*(r)Sh	Retain	RtN
Repulsive	R*Pu*(r)Sf	Retake	RtK
Reputation	R*P*Tshn	Retaliate	Rt*L*T
Request	RKlst	Retaliation	Rt*L*shn
Requiem	RKlAM	Retard	RTrt
Require-ment	RWr	Retentive	RtNTf
Requisite	RKlsT	Reticule	RtK*l*
Requisition	RKlsshn	Retire-ment	RTr
Requite	RKlT	Retract	RTr
Rescind	RSnt	Retraction	RTrshn
Research	Rs*R*Ch	Retreat	RTrT
Resemble-ance	RsM	Retribution	RTrBshn
*Resent	RsNt	Retrospect	RTrsPK
Reserve-ation	RsR	Return	RRn
Reservoir	RsR *V*	Reveal	RVl
*Reside	RsD	Revelation	RVlshn
Residuum	RsDuM	*Reveille	RVlY
Resign	RsN	*Revelry	RVl*R*
Resignation	RsG	Revenge	R *V*nJ
Resist-ance	RsSt	Revenue	R*V*N
Resolute	Rs*l*	Reverence	RfRns
Resolution	RsShn	Reverend-t	RfRnt

Reverse	RfRs	Rosette	RZt
Revert	RfRd	Rostrum	RsRM
Revive-al	RVf	Rotary	RtR
Revivify	RVF	Rotunda	RTnD
Revocable	RVKB	Rowel	Row$l$
Revolt	RVlt	Royal-ty	Rawi
Revolution	RVlshn	Rudiment-ary	R^{3}tM
Revolutionary	RVlsNR	*Ruin	Rn
Revolutionist	RVlshnst	Ruinous	RnS
Revolutionize	RVlshns	Rule	Rl
Revolve-r	RVlf	Ruminate-ion	RMN
*Revulsion	RVlshn;eu	*Rumor	RMR
Reward	RwR	Rural	RRl
Rhapsody	RPsoD	Rustic-ate	RsK
Rhetoric-al	R^{1}trK	Rusticity	RsTsT
Rhetorician	RtrEShn		
Rheumatic	R-M	**S**	
Rich	RCh		
Ride	RD	Sabbath	SBTh
Ridicule	RDKl	Saber	sBR
Ridiculous	RDKls	Sacrament	sKRM
Rifle	RFl	Sacred	sKD
Right	Rt	Sacredness	sKDns
*Right-angle	Rt^{3}Ng	Sacrifice	sKRFs
Righteous	RChs	Sacrificial	sKRF
Riot	RT	Sacrilege	sKRlJ
Ritual	RChl	Sad	sD
Rival	Rtl	Sadducee	sJcS
Rivalry	RtlR	Safe	Sf
River	RfR	Safety	SfE
Road	RD	Safety-valve	SfVf
Roar	RR	Sagacious	sGAShs
*Rob-ber	RB	Sail	sL
Rock	RK	Sailor	sLR
Rogue	RoG	Saint	Snt
Romantic	RMnK	Salary	sLR
Roseate	RZt	Sale	Sl
		Salient	sLNd

LIGHT-LINE SHORTHAND. 159

Saliva	sLV	Sausage	SsZh
Saloon	sLN	Savage	sVJ
Salt	sLd	Save-ior	Sf
Saltpetre	sLPtr	Sawyer	SY
Salubrious	sLuBs	Scaffold	sKFlt
Salubrity	sLuBti	Scarcity	sKRsti
*Salutary	sLuTR	Scenery	SnR
Salute	sLT	School	sKl
Salvage	sLVJ	School-house	sKlows
Same	sM	Schooner	sKnR
Sample	SmP	*Science	SnS
Sanctification	sKtFshn	Scientific	SnF
Sanctify	sKtF	Scorn	sKRn
Sanctimonious	sKtMNs	Scornful	sKRnF
Sanction	sNgshn	Scripture	sKP
Sanctity	sKTT	Scrofula	sKFla
Sanctuary	sKChr	Scruple	sKPl
Sanctum	sKtM	Scrutiny	sKtN
Sand	Snt	Sculpture	sKlP
Sandal	Snt$l$	Sculptor	sKlPtr
Sandstone	SntsN	Scurrility	sKRLT
Sandwich	Snt$w$Sh	Seal	sL
Sanguify	sNgF	Search	sRCh
Sanguine	sNgwN	Season	SsN
Sanguineous	sNgwNs	Seaworthy	SwRDh
Sanitary	sNtR	Secede	SSt
Sanity	Snt$i$	Seceder	SSeu
Sapling	sPlNg	Secession	SSshn
Saponaceous	sPnAShs	Seclude	sKD
Sarcophagus	sRKGs	Seclusion	sKshn
Sardonic	sRDnK	Second-hand	sKnNd
Satanic	sTnK	Secret-e	sKT
Satyr	StR	Secretary	sKTR
Satisfy-action-actory	sTsF	Secretion	sKshn
Saturate	sChR	Secular	sKLR
Saturation	sChRshn	Secure	sK^s
Saucer	SsR	Security	sKT

Sedative	sDTt	Sequestrate	sKWsRT
Seductive	sDtV	Serenade	sRNd
Seed	sD	Serene	sRn
Seen	Sn	Serenity	sRnT
Segregate	sGG	Serious	Srs
Seizure	SsY	Sermon	sRMn
Seldom	sLDm	Serpent	SrPnt
Select	SlK	Servant	SrVnt
Self-denial	s²DNl	Serve	Srf
Self-esteem	s²StM	Service	SrVs
Self-evident	s² VD	Servile-ity	Srf$l$
Selfish	s²Sh	Servitude	SrfTt
Self-love	s²l(u)V	Session	Sshn
Self-will	s²l(u)	Set	St
Sell	Sl	Settee	StE
Seminal	sMNl	Settle	Stl
Seminary	sMnR	Settlement	StlM
Senate	sNt	Sever	SfR
*Senator	sNtr	Several	Sf
Senatorial	sNtRl	Severe-ity	SfR
*Send	Snt	Sexual	sKShl
Senior	SnY	Shall	Sh³
Sensation	SnSshn	Shame	ShcM
Sense	Sns	Shampoo	Shm$P$u
Sensible	Sns$B$	Shank	ShNgK
Sensitive	SnsV	Shelf	Shlf
Sensual	SnShl(r)	Shepherd	ShPrt
Sensuality	SnShT	Sheriff	ShrF
*Sent	sNt	Shield	Shlt
Sentiment-al	sNtM	Shingle	ShNgl
Sentinel	SntNl	*Ship	ShP
*Sentry	sNTr	*Shipment	ShP
Separate	sPRT	Shirk	ShRK
Separation	sPR	Shirt	ShRt
Sepulcher	sPKR	Short-hand	Shrnt
Sequel	sKwL	Should	"should"
Sequence	sKWs	Shoulder	Shltr

LIGHT-LINE SHORTHAND. 161

*Shovel	ShVl	Size	Ss
Shriek	Sh*R*K	Skillful	sK*lF*'l
*Shuttle	Sh*tU*	Skinflint	sKNFlnt
Sickle	sK*l*	Skittish	sKTSh
*Side	sD	Slander	sLnt*R*
Sift	Sft	Slate	sLd
*Sight	St	Slaughter-house	sLRHs
Sign	Sn	Slave	sLv
Signal	sG	Slavery	sLR
Signify-icance-icant	sGn*F*	Slavish	sLvs
Signification	sGn*F*shn	Sled	s*l*D
Silent	s*L*N	*Slight	s*l*T
Silk	s*L*K	Slit	sLd
Sylvan	s*L*Vn	Sloven	sL*V*n
Silver	SlVr	Slumber	sLMr
Similar-ity	sM¹	Smart	sMrd
Simple-y	Sm*P*	*Smith	SmTh
Simpleton	Sm*P*Tn	Smoke	sMK
Simplicity	Sm*P*st*i*	*Smooth	SmDh
Simplification	Sm*P*Fshn	Smother	sMDhr
Simplify	Sm*P*F	*Snag	sNcG
Simultaneous	sM*lT*n	*Snake	sNK
Sin	sN	Snatch	sNCh
Since	Sns	Sneer	sN*R*
Sincere-ity	SnS*R*	Snort	sNrd
Sinew	sNY	Soar	sor
Single	sNg	Sober	sB*R*
Singular	sNg*R*	Sobriety	sB*R*T
Singularity	sNg*R*T	Sociable	sSh*B*
Sinister	sNst*R*	*Social	sShl
Sink	sNgK	Society	SS
Sinuous	sNYs	Sofa	SF
Sir	s*R*	Soft	Sft
Sirup	s*R*P	Soil	s*L*
Sister	Sst*R*	Soiree	Sl*R*A
Sit	St	Sojourn	sJRn
Situate-ion	sCh¹	Solace	s*L*s

*Soldier	SlZh	Sound	Snt
*Soldiery	SlZh*R*	Source	Srs
Sole	Sl	Southeast	sThst
Solemn	s*L*M	Southern	sDhn
Solicit	Slst	Southward	sTh*w*R
Solicitation	SlstShn	Southwest	sTh*w*st
Solicitor	Slst*R*	Sovereign	SfRn
Solicitous	SlstS	Sovereignty	SfRn*ti*
Solicitude	SlstD	Spangle	sPNg*l*
Solid	s*L*D	Spanish	sPNSh
Soliloquy	s*Li*K	Speaker	sPKR
*Solo	SL	Speedy	sPti
Solstice	SlstS	Spendthrift	s*P*nThf
Soluble	Slu*B*	Sphere	sF*R*
Solution	Slshn	Spirit	sPt
Solvable	SlfABl	Spiritual	sPCbl
Solve	Slf	Spittoon	sPtuN
Solvent	SlfNt	Splendid	sPnD
Somebody	sMBt	Splendor	sPntr
*Something	SmTh	Sprain	sPrn
Sometimes	sMMs	Spring	sPNg
Somnambulist	sMnMBst	Squad	sKD
Somnolent	sMNlNt	Squalid	sK*l*D
Son	Sn	Squander	sKntR
Sonata	sNT	Square	sKR
Soon	Sn	Squash	sK*w*(r)Sh
Sophistry	SFst*R*	Squat	sK*w*(l)T
Soprano	sP*R*N	Squaw	sK*wa*w
Sorcerer	s*R*sR*R*	Squeeze	sK*ws*
Sorcery	s*R*sR	Squirm	sK*w*RM
Sordid	s*R*Dt	Squirrel	sKR*l*
Sore	sor	Staff	sTf
Sorrow	s*R*	*Staid	sTt
Sorry	s*R*	Stain	sTn
Sort	s*R*T	Stalactite	st*L*KTt
Sot	St	Stale	stL
*Soul	Sl	Stall	stL

Stammer	stMr	Stomach	stMK
Stand	sTnt	Stone	sTn
Standard	sTnRd	Storehouse	st*R*ows
Stanza	sTnZ	Storm	st*R*M
Star	st*R*	Story	st*R*i
Start	st*R*T	Stove	sTf
Starve	st*R*f	*Stowage	sTcJ
State	stT	Straddle	strD*l*
Statement	stTcM	Straight	strT
Station	sTshn	Strand	strNt
Stationary	sTsN*R*	Strange	strJ
Statistics	stTsKs	Stranger	strJR
Statuary	stChR*i*	Strangle	strNg*l*
Statue	stChu	Strangulation	strNg*l*Shn
Stature	stChR	Stratagem	strTcJM
Stave	sTf	Strawberry	strB*R*
*Steady	stD	Stray	sTr
Steal	stL	Strenuous	strNYs
Steam	stM	Stricken	strKN
Steamer	stMr	Stroll	str*L*
Steelyard	stLY	Stubborn	stBn
Steeple	stP*l*	Student	stDnt
Stencil	sTs*L*	Study	stD
Stereotype	st*R*TP	Stuff	sTf
Sterile	st*Rl*	Stultify	sT*lt F*
Stern	st*R*n	Stupendous	stPnDs
Stethoscope	stThosKP	Stutter	sTtr
Steward	sTRd	Style	stL
Stiff	sTf	Suasion	Slshn
Still	stL	Suavity	SlfEE
Stilt	stLd	Sub-committee	sB-T
Stimulant	stM*l*Nd	Subdue	sBtu
Stimulate-ation	stM*l*A	*Subject	sB
Stipulate-ion	stP*L*	*Subjection	sBshn
Stoic	stoK	Subjective	sBf
Stoicism	stosM	*Subjugate-ion	sBJG
Stolid	st*L*D	*Sublime-ity	sBM

Submit	sBmT	Sulphuret	s*L F*rT
Submission	sBmshn	Sulphuric	s*L F*rK
Submissive	sBms*V*	Sultan	s*L T*n
Subordinate	sBtNd	Summer	sMr
Subpœna	sB*P*	Sumptuous	sMPChs
Subsequent	sBsKnt	Sun	Sn
Subserve	sBs*R*	Superannuated	sPNY
Subservient	sBs*R V*nt	Supercilious	sPSls
Subsist	sBSst	Supereminent	sPMNNd
Substantial	sBsNSh	Supererogation	sP*R*Gshn
Subterfuge	sBtr*F*J	Superexcellent	sPKsNd
Subterranean	sBtrNN	Superficial	sPFSh
Subtract	sBTr	Superintend-ent	sPnTnt
Subtraction	sBTrshn	Superintendence	sPnTnNs
Subvert	sB*V*rT	Superior	sP*R R*
Succeed	sKsD	Supernatural	sPnCh
Success-ful	SsS	Superstitious	sPsTShs
Succession	SsShn	Supervisor	sP *V*sR
Successive	SsSf	Supper	sP*R*
Successor	SsS*R*	Supply	sPl
Succinct	sKsNg	Support	sP*R*d
Suffer	SFr	Suppress	sPs
Suffice	SFs	Suppression	sPshn
Sufficiency-t	SFSh	Suppurate-ion	sPu*R*
Suffix	s*F*Ks	*Supreme	sPm
Suffocate-ion	s*F*K	Supremacy	sPmS
Suffuse	SFs	Sure	Shr
Sugar	ShGr	Surety	ShrtE
Suggest-ion	sJst	Surf	s*R*f
Suggestive	sJsTf	Surface	SrFs
Suicide	SSt	Surmise	s*R*Ms
*Suit	St	*Surpass	s*R*Ps
Suitable	SBl	Surplus	s*R*Ps
Suitor	Str	*Surprise	sPs
Sulky	s*L*K	Surrender	s*R*nt*R*
Sulphate	s*L*Ft	Surreptitious	s*R*PShs
Sulphur	s*L F*r	Survey	SrV

Survive-or	SrVf	Sympathy-etic	SmPTh
Susceptible	SsPB	Symptom	SmPtM
Suspect	SsP	Symptomatic	SmPt-M
Suspend	SsPnt	Synagogue	sNGG
Suspicion	SsPshn	Synonymous	sNNMs
Suspicious	SsPsS	Synopsis	sNPsS
Sustain	SsN	Syringe	sRnJ
Sustentation	SsNShn	*System	Sst
Suture	sChR	Systematic	Sst-M
Swab	SlB	Systemize	SstZ
Swaddle	Sltl		
Swag	SlcG	**T**	
Swain	swN	Tabernacle	TBnK
Swale	swL	*Table	TBl
Swallow	swL	*Tableau	TBlo
Swamp	SlmP	Taciturnity	TsTRnti
Swarm	SlRM	Tactics	TKKs
Swarth	SlRTh	Take	T^q
Swath	SlTh	Talent	TlNd
Sway	sW	Tambourine	TmBRN
Swear	SlR	Tame	TcM
Sweat	Slt	Tanner	TnR
Sweep	SlP	Tantalize	TntIs
*Sweet	sT	Tantalization	TntIsShn
Swell	swL	Tardy	TrD
Swerve	SlRf	Tariff	TRv
*Swift	Slft	Tarnish	TRnSh
Swill	swL	Tartar	TRdr
Swim	SlM	Tattle	Ttl
Swindle	Slntl	*Tax	Ts^3
Swindler	SlntR	Taxable	Ts^{3}B
Swing	SlNg	Taxation	Ts^{3}shn
*Switch	SlCh	Technical	TKnK
Switchman	SlChmN	Te Deum	TDm
Syllable	SlB	Telegram	TlGrm
Sylph	sLv	Telegraph	TlGrf
Symmetry	sMTr	Telescope	TlsKP

Temerity	TMrT	*Thanksgiving	Th¹NgsG
*Temper	TmP	That	Dh³
*Temperament	TmPM	The	¡¹
Temperance	TmPns	Theater	ThTr
*Temperate	TmP*R*	Their	Dbr
*Temperature	TmPChr	*Theism	This*M*
Tempest	TmPst	*Theist-ical	This*t*
Tempestuous	*T*mPsChs	Them	Dhm
Templar	TmP*LR*	Themselves	Dhms
Temple	TmP*l*(u)	Thenceforth	DhsFTh
Temporal	TmP*l*	Theodolite	ThawD*l*T
*Temporary	TmRR	Theoretical	Th¹*R*K
Tempt	TnPt	Theory	Th*R*
Temptation	TmPshn	Therapeutics	Th*R*PtKs
Tempter	TmPtR	There	R³
*Tenable	TnABl	Thereabout	R³*B*
Tenacious	TNShs	Thereafter	R³*F*
Tenacity	TNst*i*	Thereat	*R*³T
Tendency	TnNS	Thereby	R³B
Tenor	TnR	Therefor	R³F
Tergiversation	TrGRSshn	Therefore	R³Fr
Term-inate	TRM	Therein	R³n
Termination	TRMshn	Thereof	R³F:aw
Terminus	TRMnS	Thereon	R³ "on"
Terrestrial	TrstR*l*	Thereupon	R³P
Terrific	TR*F*K	Therewith	R³*w*
Territory	TrTR	Thermometer	ThrMM
*Testament	TsMd	These	is¹
Testator	TsTtr	Thick	ThcK
Testatrix	TsTtKs	Thievish	Thf*E*Sh
Testify	Ts*F*	Thing	Th¹
*Testimony	TsM	Think	Th¹
Texture	TsChR	Third	Thrt
Than	N³	Thither	Dhtr
Thank	Th³	Thou	Dh³
Thankful	Th³f	Thousand	Th³
Thankfulness	Th³fNs	Thralldom	Thr*l*M

Threshold	ThrSht	*Torment	TRMnt
Thrifty	ThrfE	Tornado	TrnD:o
Throughout	ThrT	Torrent	TRnt
Thump	Thm*P*	Torture	TrChr
Thunderstruck	Thnt*R*sK	Total	TT*l*
Thwart	Thl*R*T	Toward	Trt
Ticket	TK	Township	TnSh
Till	Tl	*Tract	Trt³
Timber	TmB	Tractable	Trt³ABl
Time	M¹	Tractile	Trt³*l*
*Timekeeper	TcMKP	*Traction	Tr³Kshn
*Timely	TMl	Trade	Trt
Timepiece	TcMPs	*Trader	Trtr
Timid	TmD	Trade-wind	Trt*w*N
Timorous	TMrs	Tradition	TrDshn
Tincture	TnKChr	Tragedy-ic	TrcJ
*Tingle	TNgl	*Trait-or	TrT
*Tinkle	TnK*l*	Tramp	TrmP
Tiptop	TPtP	Tranquil	TrnK*l*
Tire	TR	Transact	TrsK
Titillate	TT*L*	Transaction	TrsKshn
Title	T*L*	Transatlantic	TrsTntK
Tittle-tattle	TT*tl*	Transcend	TrsNd
To	"to"	Transcendent	TrsNN
To-day	"to"D	Transcript	TrsKP
Together	G²	*Transfer	Trs²*F*
Told	Tlt	*Transform	Trs¹*F*r
Tolerable	T*LR*B	Transformation	Trs¹*F*rshn
Tolerance-t	T*LR*N	Transgressor	TrsGsR
Tolerate-ion	T*LR*	Transient	Trshnt .
Tomahawk	TmHK	Transit	TrsT
Tomb	TcM	Transition	Trsshn
To-morrow	M¹R	Translate-ion	Trs*L*
Tonsil	TNs*l*	Transparency-t	TrsP*R*
Too	T³	Transpiration	TrsP*R*shn
Took	T³	Transpire	TrsP*R*
Torch	TRCh	Transplant	TrsPnt

Transport-ation	TrsP*R*	Tunnel	TNl
Transverse	Trs*V*s	Turbulence	TrBns
Travel	Tr*V*l	Turbulent	TrBnt
Travesty	Trfst	Turf	TRv
Treachery	TrChri	Turgid	TRJ
*Treasure	TrsR	Turgidity	TRJT
*Treasurer	TrsR*R*	Turn	Trn
*Treasury	TrsR*i*	Turnip	TRn*P*
Tremble	TrmB	Turpentine	TrPnTn
Tremendous	TrcMnS	Turpitude	TrPtD
Tremor	TrMr	Turtle	Trt*l*
Tremulous	TrMls	Tutor	Ttr³
Trepidation	TrPtshn	Twain	TwN
Trial	Tr*L*	Twang	TlNg
Triangle	TrNgl	Tweezers	TlsRs
Tribulation	TrBlshn	*Twice	Tls
Tribunal	TrBNl	Twine	TwN
Trillion	Tr*l*N	Twinkle	TlnK*l*
Trinity	TrnT	Twirl	TlR*l*
Triplicate	TrPKT	Twist	Tlst
Triumph	Trm*F*	Two	T³
Trivial	TrfE*l*	Tympanum	TmPnM
Trowsers	TrsRs	Typhoid	T*F*t
Truant	TrNd	Tyranny	TRN
Trump	TrmP	Tyrant	TRnt
Trumpet	TrmPt		
*Trustee	TrsT	**U**	
*Trusty	Trsti		
*Tub	T*B*	Ubiquity	YBKT
*Tube	TuB	Ulcer	Ls*R*
Tuition	TShn	Ultimate	*L*M
Tumble	TmB	Ultimo	*L*M
Tumbler	TmB*R*	Ultra	*L*T
Tumult	TMlt	Unaccented	nKsN*t*
Tumultuous	TMlts	Unaccompanied	nKNd
*Tune	Tn³	Unaccustomed	nKsMd
*Tuner	Tn³R	Unalterable	n*LR*B
		Unanimous	YnNMs

Unanswerable	nNsRBl	Unengaged	NnG
*Unavoidable	N *VB*	Unenlightened	NNltN
Uncertain	Ns*RT*	Unequal	NKl
Unchangeable	nChB	Unequivocal	nKfoK
Uncivil	NsV	*Uneven	N *VN*
Uncomfortable	nF*RT*	Unexceptionable	nKsPsN*B*
Uncommon	nK	Unexpected	nKsPK
Unconcerned	NSrnt	Unfaithful	nFThf
Unconditional	NDshn	Unfavorable	nFB
Unconnected	N-K	Unforeseen	NFrSn
Unconscious	NShs	Unfortunate	N*F*ChnT
Unconstitutional	N'sTshn	Unfurl	NFr*l*
Unctuous	NgChs	Ungracious	NGrAShs
Uncultivated	NKlt *V*	Unguarded	nGR*t*
Under	Nt³	Uniform	Yn*F*R
Underbrush	NBrSh	Uniformity	Yn*F*T
Undercurrent	NtKRnt	Unimportant	nMP
Underground	NtGnt	Unintcrested	nNtst
Undergrowth	NtGcTh	Uninteresting	nNtst-*e*
Underhanded	NHnt	Uninterrupted	NnTPt*t*
Underline	Nt³*l*N	Union	YnN
Underneath	Nt³NTh	*Unit	YNd
Understand-ing	NsTnt	Unite	YnT
Understood	NsTt	*Unity	YnT'
Undertake	NtT	Universal	Yn *V*s
Undertaker	NtTKr	Universality	Yn *V*s*l*T
Undertook	NtTu	Universe	Yn *V*s
Underwriter	NtRR	University	Yn *V*sT
Undeviating	nDf*E*T	Unknown	NNn
Undivided	nD *Vt*	Unless	Nls
Undoubted	nD*t*	Unlike	NlK
*Undoubtedly	nD*L*	Unlimited	nLM
Undulate	NJlT	Unlovely	nLVl
Undulation	NJlshn	Unlucky	NlKi
*Unduly	nDu*L*	Unmannerly	NmNr
Unearthly	N*R*Th	Unmindful	NMnF
Uneducated	nJK*t*	Unnatural	*eu*NChr

Unnecessary	*eu*NsR	Valuable	VlB
Until	NTl	*Valuation	Vl³Shn
Untimely	nTMl	Value	Vl
Untiring	NTr-*e*	Valve	Vlf
Unto	nT²	Valvular	VlV*l*R
Unutterable	nTRB*l*	Vampire	VMP*R*
Unwary	N*w*R*i*	Vanish	VnSh
Unwilling	N*l*(d)-*e*	Vanity	*V*nT
Unwitting	N*w*-*e*	Vanquish	*V*nKs
Unworthy	NDh	Variable	V*R*B
Unwritten	NrdN	Variance	V*R*Ns
Upright	P*R*T	Variation	V*R*shn
Upward	P*w*R	Variegated	V*R*G
Us	s²	Variety	V*R*T
Usage	YsJ	Various	V*R*s
Use	Ys	Varnish	V*R*nSh
Useful	Ys*F*	Vehement	VMnt
Useless	Ys*l*s	Vehicle	VHKl
Usual	Zh³	Velocity	Vlst*i*
Usurp	YsR*P*	Venality	VNlT
Usury	YsR	Vendee	Vnt*i*
Utensil	YTs*l*	Veneer	VnR
Utility	YTT	Venerable	VnR*B*
Utmost	TcMst	Ventilate	VntLt
Utter	TR	Ventriloquist	Vnt*R*Kst
Utterly	TRL	Venture	*V*nChR
		Venue	VnY
V		Veracious	VrAShs
Vacillate	VSL	Veracity	Vr*A*st*i*
Valediction	*V*lDshn	Verdant	V*R*Dnt
Valedictory	*V*lDR	Verdict	*V*rK
Valentine	*V*lntN	Verdure	V*R*Jr
Valet	*V*lT	Verify	VrF
Valid	*V*lD	Veritable	V*R*TB
Validity	*V*lDT	Verity	Vr*i*T
Valley	Vl*i*	Vernacular	*V*rnK*l*R
Valor	Vl*R*	Vernal	VrNl

LIGHT-LINE SHORTHAND. 171

Versatility	VrSTlT	Virtue	VrCh
Verse	Vrs	Virulent	VrlNd
Versification	VrsFshn	Visible	VsB
Versify	VrsF	Visionary	VsNR
Version	Vrshn	Visit	Vst
Vertebra	VrTB	Vista	Vst$A$
Vertex	VrTKs	Vital	VTl
Vertical	VrTKl	Vitality	VTT
Very	V^2	Vitrefy	VtRF
Vestibule	VstBl	Vituperate	VTPt
Vestry	Vst$R$i	Vituperation	VTPshn
Vesture	VsChR	Vivacity	VVst$i$
Veterinary	VTRnR	Viva Voce	VVS
Veto	VT	Vivify	VVF
Vicinity	VSnt	Vizier	VZh
Vicissitude	VSstD	Vocabulary	VKBLR
Victim	VKm	Vociferate	VsFR
Victimize	VKmIs	Void	Vt
Victor	VKeu	Volatile	VlTl
Victory	VKR	Volcano	VlKN
Victuals	Vtls	Volition	Vlshn
Vigilance	VJns	Voluble	Vlu$B$
Vigilant	VJnt	Volume	VlM
*Vignette	VnYT	*Voluntary	Vlnt$R$i
Village	VlJ	*Volunteer	Vlnt$R$
Villain	VlN	Voluptuous	VlPChs
Vindicate	VntK	*Voracious	VoRShs
Vindictive	VntKTf	Vortex	VrTKs
*Vineyard	VnYt	*Votary	VtR
*Viol	$V$$ll$	Vote	Vt
Viola	VoL	*Voter	Vtr
Violate	VlA	Vowel	Vl
Violation	Vl'Shn	Vulcanize	VlKnIs
Violence	Vlns	Vulgar	VlG
Violent	VlNt	Vulgarity	VlGT
Violin	VlN	Vulnerable	VlNBl
Virgin	VrJn	Vulture	VlChR

W

Wade	wD	Weapon	w(r)Pn
Wail	wL	Weary	wR
Waist	Wst	Weather	w(r)Dhr
Wait	wT	Weave	w(l)V
Wall	wL	Web	w(r)B
Wallet	wLT	Ween	wN
Wall-flower	wLF¹R	Weep	w(r)P
Wallow	wL	Welcome	wLK
Waltz	wLds	Welfare	wLFr
Wan	wN	Well	wL
Wand	wNt	Welsh	wLSh
Wander	wN¹R	Welter	wLR
Wane	wN	Went	wNt
Want	wNt	West	Wst
Wanton	wNtN	Western	WsRN
War	wR	Westward	WsRt
Warble	wRB	Whale	Hwl
Ward	wRt	Wharf	Hwv
Wardrobe	wRtRB	Wharfinger	HwvJR
Ware	wR	What	T¹
Warehouse	wRows	Whatever	Tf¹
Warm	wM	Whatsoever	T¹sV
Warmth	wMTh	Wheat	HwT
*Warn	wRn	Wheel	Hwl
*Warrant	wRN	When	wN¹
*Warrantee	wRnT	Whence	Hwns
*Warrior	wRR	Whensoever	wN¹Sf
Wary	wR	Whenever	wN¹f
Was	Z³	Where	w³(r)
Wasp	WsP	Whereat	w²·T²
Waste	Wst	Wherefore	w³Fr
Water	W¹	Wherein	w²(l)N
Wave	w(l)V	Whereof	w³F
Waver	w(r)Vr	Whereupon	w³P
We	w¹(r)	Wheresoever	w²Sf
Wealth	wLTh	Whereto	w²(l) " to "
		Wherever	w³Vr

Wherewith	w^2w	Window	wND
Whether	Hw²	Wine	wN
Which	Ch²	Wing	w(l)Ng
Whichever	Chf²	Wink	wNK
Whiffletree	HwFlTi	Winner	wNR
While	wL	Winter	wNtr
Whim	HwM	Wipe	wP
Whine	Hwn	Wire	wR
Whip	HwP	Wisdom	WsM
Whirl	HwRl	Wish	Sh¹
Whirlwind	HwRwNt	Wisp	WsP
Whisper	HwsP	Wit	wT
White	Hwd	With	w¹(r)
Whitewash	HwdSh	Withdraw	Dh¹Dr
Whithersoever	HwDhrSf	Wither	w(r)Dhr
Who	H²	Withheld-hold	w¹(r)Hlt
Whole	Hl	Within	w(l)N¹
Wholesale	Hlsl	Without	w(l)T²
Whom	H²	*Withstand	wSnt³
Whose	Hs²	Wizard	WsRt
Why	Hw¹	Wolf	wLv
Wide	wD	Woman	wMn³
Widow	wD	Womanhood	wMnHt
Width	wDTh	Women	wMn¹
Wield	wLd	Wonder-ful	wN¹R
Wife	w(l)F	Wondrous	wNDrs
Wigwam	wGwM	Wood	wD
Wild	wLD	Woodland	wDlN
Wilderness	wLRNs	Wool	wL
Willful	l¹(d)Fl	Woolen	wLN
Will	l¹(d)	Word	Rt
Willingness	l¹(d)-Ns	Wordy	RtE
Willow	wL	Work	w(l)R
Wiley	wL	Workmanlike	wRMNlK
Win	wN	World	eu²
Winch	wNCh	Worldliness	eu²Ns
Wind	wNt	Worldly	eu²l

Worm	wRM	Year	u¹(u)
Worn	wRn	Yearly	u¹l
Worry	wRi	Yellow	YL
Worse	wRs	Yes	Ys
*Worship	wRSh	Yesterday	YsD
Worshipful	wRShf	Yet	u²(u)
*Worshipper	wRShP	Yield	Yt
Worst	wRst	Yonder	YntR
Worsted	wRstt	You	u³(d)
Worth	Th²	Young	Ng
Worthless	Thls	Younger	NgR
Worthy	Dh²	Youngster	NgstR
Would	w²(l)	Your	Y³
Wound	wNt	Yourself	Ys³
Wrangle	RNgl	Youth	u(u)Th
Wrinkle	RnKl	Youthful	uThf
*Write	Rt		
*Writer	RR		Z
Writing	RtNg	Zealous	ZLs
Written	RtN	Zebra	ZBr
		Zenith	ZnTh
	Y	Zephyr	ZFr
Yacht	YT	Zero	ZR
Yankee	YnK	Zigzag	ZGsG
Yard	Yt	Zinc	ZNgK
Yarn	YRn	Zouave	ZV
Ye	Y	Zymotic	Z-M

MONTHS.

January	JnR	July	Jl
February	FB	August	Gst
March	MRCh	September	sPtM
April	PrL	October	KTB
May	M	November	NfM
June	Jn	December	DsM

DAYS OF THE WEEK.

Sunday	sND	Thursday	ThRsD
Monday	MnD	Friday	FrD
Tuesday	TsD	Saturday	sTD
Wednesday	wNsD		

GRAND DIVISIONS OF THE EARTH.

Europe	YP	North America	NrMr
Asia	ASh	South America	sThM
Africa	FrK	Australia	STrL
America	MrK		

PRINCIPAL COUNTRIES, ETC., OF THE WORLD.

Abyssinia	BsNA	Guatemala	GTMl
Algeria	LJR	Guinea	GN
Amazon	MsN	Hindoostan	HnDsTn
Arabia	RB	India	nDiA
Bolivia	BLV	Ireland	RlN
Brazil	Brs$L$	Italy	TL
Canada	KnD	Jamaica	JMK
Cape Colony	KPKlN	Japan	JPn
Central America	sNTrMr	Mexico	MKsK
Chili	ChL	Morocco	MRK
China	ChN	New Brunswick	NBrnsK
Denmark	DnMRK	Newfoundland	NFnt$l$N
East Indies	StNDs	New Grenada	NGrnD
Egypt	JPt	New Zealand	NZlN
England	Ngnt	Nicaragua	NKrG
Ethiopia	ThP	Norway	NRW
France	Frns	Nova Scotia	NVsKSh
Germany	JRMN	Ontario	NTR
Gibraltar	JBRLR	Palestine	PLsTn
Great Britain	GrBtN	Patagonia	PtGN
Greece	Grs	Persia	PRSh

176　　　LIGHT–LINE SHORTHAND.

Peru	P*R*u	Sumatra	sMTr
Prussia	PrSh	Sweden	SltN
Russia	RSh	Tasmania	TsMN
Scotland	sK*l*N	Tehuantepec	TwNPK
Sahara	sHR	Tripoli *	TrP*L*
Saxony	sKsN	Tunis	TNs
Siberia	sB*R*a	Turkey	TRK
Sierra Nevada	s*Rn V*D	United States	Ys
Soudan	SDn	Venezuela	VnZL
Spain	sPn	Yucatan	YKTn

STATES AND TERRITORIES.

Alabama	*L*BM	Mississippi	MsSs*P*
Alaska	*L*(b)sK	Missouri	MsR
Arizona	*R*sN	Montana	MnTN
Arkansas	*R*Knss	Nebraska	NBrsK
California	Kl*F*r	Nevada	N*V*D
Colorado	K*LR*D	New Hampshire	NHmSh
Connecticut	KNtK	New Jersey	nJRZ
Dakota	DKT	New Mexico	N²MsK
Delaware	DlW	New York	N¹Y
District of Columbia	DsKmB	North Carolina	NKrN
Florida	Fl*R*D	Ohio	HI
Georgia	JrJ	Oregon	*R*Gn
Illinois	*L*N	Pennsylvania	Ps*V*N
Indiana	NtN	Rhode Island	Rt*L*N
Indian Territory	NtNTrTR	South Carolina	sThKrN
Iowa	*I*W	Tennessee	TnS
Kansas	Knss	Texas	TKss
Kentucky	KntK	Utah	YT
Louisiana	LsN	Vermont	VrMut
Maine	Mn	Virginia	*V*rJN
Maryland	MRLnt	Washington Territory	ShTTR
Massachusetts	MsChsTs		
Michigan	MSh	Wisconsin	WsKsN
Minnesota	MNsT	Wyoming	WmNg

CITIES AND TOWNS.

Acapulco	KP*L*K	Cleveland	Kl*V*lnt
Albany	*L*BcN	Columbus	KlMBs
Alexandria	*L*Ks.NDr	Concord	KnKRd
Amsterdam	Ms*R*Dm	Constantinople	KsTntNPl
Athens	Thns	Copenhagen	KPnHGn
Atlanta	T*L*nT	Council Bluffs	Ks*L*Bfs
Auburn	awBrn	Cork	KRK
Augusta	GsT	Denver	Dn*V*R
Austin	StN	Detroit	DRawi
Baltimore	BltMR	Dresden	DrsDn
Bangor	BnGR	Dublin	DBln
Bath	*B*Th	Edinburgh	DnBG
Belfast	B*l*(u)*F*st	Fall River	F*lR*v*R*
Benicia	BNSh	Florence	Fl*R*Ns
Berlin	B*RlN*	Frankfort	*F*rnK*F*rT
Bethlehem	BThlM	Fredericksburg	*F*rDKsBG
Beyrout	B*R*T	Galena	G*L*N
Birmingham	BrmNgM	Galveston	Gl*V*stN
Bombay	BmB	Geneva	J*N V*
Boston	BsTn	Gettysburg	GTsBG
Brattleboro	Brt*l*B*R*	Gibraltar	JB*RLR*
Bristol	BrsT*l*	Glasgow	GlsG
Brooklyn	BrK*l*N	Grass Valley	Grs*V*li
Brussels	Brs*l*s	Halifax	Hl*l*Fs
Buenos Ayres	BwNsRs	Hamburg	HMBG
Buffalo	BFl	Harrisburg	HRsBG
Burlington	Br*L*;Tn	Hartford	HrdFt
Cairo	KRo	Havre	H*V*r
Cambridge	KmBJ	Hong Kong	HnKNg
Canton	KnTn	Honolulu	HNlL
Cape Town	KPTn	Indianapolis	NtNPls
Catskill	KsK*l*	Jackson	JKsN
Charleston	Chr*l*sTn	Jacksonville	JKsNVl
Chicago	ShKG	Jefferson	J*F*rsN
Cincinnati	SnSnt*i*	Jerusalem	JRsM

Key West	KWst	New Orleans	N*RI*Ns
Kingston	KNgsN	New York	NY
Lafayette	L*F*T	Niagara	N*I*GR
La Paz	LPs	Panama	PnM
Lima	LM	Paris	P*R*s
Limerick	LMrK	Philadelphia	Fl*lF*
Lincoln	LnKn	Placerville	PlsRVl
Little Rock	L*R*K	Plymouth	PlMcTh
Liverpool	LVrPl	Portland	Prt*LN*
London	*l*(d)NN	Porto Rico	PrtRK
Los Angeles	LsNg	Providence	PrfDns
Louisville	LsV*l*	Quebec	KBK
Lowell	L*l*	Quincy	KlNS
Lynn	*l*(d)N	Raleigh	RL
Manchester	MnChstR	Richmond	RChMnt
Marblehead	MrBHd	Rio Janeiro	RJnR
Marseilles	MrSls	Rochester	RChstR
Marysville	MRsV*l*	Rome	RM
Mazatlan	MsT*lN*	Sacramento	sKRM
Melbourne	M*l*Bn	St. Louis	sNt*L*s
Memphis	MMFs	St. Petersburg	sNPsBG
Milwaukee	Ml*w*K	Salem	s*L*M
Mobile	MB*l*	Salt Lake City	s*Ll*KsT
Monterey	MntR	San Francisco	sNsK
Monte Video	MnT*V*D	San Jose	sNZ
Montgomery	MnGmR	Santa Barbara	sNBrB*R*
Montpelier	MntP*LR*	Santa Clara	sNKlR
Montreal	MntR*l*	Santa Fe	sN*F*A
Moscow	MsK	Santa Rosa	sNtRZ
Mt. Vernon	MnT*V*rNN	Saratoga	s*R*TG
Nantucket	NNtKT	Savannah	s*V*N
Napa	N*P*	Shanghai	ShNgI
Naples	NPls	Sheffield	ShF*l*t
Nashville	NShVl	Smyrna	sM*RN*
Nazareth	NsRTh	Springfield	sPNgFlt
New Bedford	NBt*F*r	Stockholm	stKM
New Haven	NHvN	Sydney	sDN

Syracuse	s*R*Ks	Vienna	*VNA*
Tallahassee	T*L*S	Virginia City	*V*rJNsT
Toledo	T*LD*	Waltham	w*L*dM
Topeka	TPK	Washington	ShTn
Utica	YTK	Washington, D. C.	ShTnDS
Vallejo	VlH	Waterloo	WLu
Valparaiso	VlPrZ	Wilmington	w*L*M;Tn
Venice	VnS	Worcester	Wst*R*
Vera Cruz	V*R*Krs	Yonkers	YnKRs
Vicksburg	*V*KsBG	Yreka	w*R*K
Victoria	*V*KTR		

MISCELLANEOUS PHRASES.

About that time	B³Dhm	At all events	T³lfNs
Above all	B*tl*	*At all times	T³]ms
Am not	MnT	At any time	T³nM
American people	M³rP*P*	At any rate	T³nRd
Are not	*R*nT	At first	T³st
Are you	*R*u	*At last	T³*l*st
As a matter of course	s²MKrs	*At least	T³lst
As far as	s*FR*s	At length	T³lTh
As fast as	sFsts	At liberty	T³B
As for	sF	At one time	T³lnM
As follows	sFs	At once	T³ns
As good as	s²Gs	At our own	T³rn
As it is	sTs	At present	T²Prs
As large as	s²Js	At right angles	T³RNgs
As long as	s²Ngs	At that time	T³Dhm
As many as	s²MNs	At the present time	T³PrsM
As much as	s²Chs	At the rate of	T³Rd
As near as	s³Nrs	At what time	T³Tm
As soon as	s³Ss	At which	T³Ch
As soon as convenient	sSsVn	But it is	"but" Ts
As soon as possible	sSs*P*	But not	"but" o
As well as	s³w*L*s	By any means	B¹nMns
At all	T³]	By no means	B¹*I*Mns

By way of	B¹Wf	Have not	H³nT
Can be done	K³BtN	He had	H¹Hd
Can have	K³f	He has	H¹Hs
Cannot	K³nT	He is not	H¹sNd
Can't	Knt	He might	HmT
Come in	K³n	He must	H¹mst
Come on	KN	He must be	H¹msB
Could not	"could"nt	He must have	HmsH
Did not	DtN	He must not	HmsN
Do not	D³nT	He said	Hst
Don't	Dnt	House of Commons	H³sKs
During this time	D³rDhsM	House of Lords	HsRts
Each other	Ch¹tr	House of Representatives	HsRs
Ever saw	V¹S		
For that purpose	FDhP	How long	H³Ng
For the purpose	FP	How many	H³mN
For the sake of	FsK	If anything	FnTh
For what	FT	If it is-has	Fts
For which	FCh	If there be	FRB
Give us	G¹s	If you	Fl
Give you	G¹u	If you are	FlR
Good many	G³mN	If you have	FlH
Go on	G³N	If you were-would	Flw
Great deal	Grl	If you will	Fll
Great many	GrmN	If your	FY
Greater than	GrN	In an	Nn(f)
Had had	HdH	In all	Nl
Had it been	HdtBn	In all cases	NlKss
Had it not	Hdtnt	In all its	Nlts
Had not	Hn(b)t	In all probability	NlPrB
Has had	s³Ht	In any	NN
Has it	s³T	In any other	NN"other"
Has not	sNt	In a short time	NShtM
Has not been	sNtN	In as much as	NsCh³s
Have been	H³n(f)	In every respect	N V RsPK
Have had	H³Hd	In him	Nm(f)
Have it	H³T	In his-us	N¹s

LIGHT-LINE SHORTHAND.

*In his life	NsF	Just about	JstB
In its	Nts	Just as good	JstsG
In my	Nm(f)	Just as long	JstsNg
*In my life	NmF	Just as well	Jstsw$L$
In order	NRR	Kingdom of Heaven	K¹fHN
In other words	NRts	Larger than	Jr³n
In our	Nr	Less than	LsN
In reality	Nrl	Let it	"let"t
In reference to	NF	Let it be	"let"tB
In regard to	NR	Let me	"let"M
In relation to	NShn	Let not	"let""no"
In respect	NsPK	Let the	"let"E
In the course	NtKRs	Let there be	"let"RB
In the first place	Nst$P$s	Let us	"let"s
In the second place	NsKPs	Let us have	"let"sH
In this matter	nDhsM	Let us not	"let"s"no"
In which	nCh	Let you	"let"u(u)
Is it	s¹T	Lighter than	LtrN
Is it not	s¹TnT	Long and short	NgnSht
Is not	s¹Nt	Long time	Ngm
Is that	s¹Dh	Lord and Saviour	R¹dSf
Is there	s¹R	Lord God	R¹G
It had	T²t	Lord Jesus Christ	RJK
It has	T²s	Many years	mNus
It is	T²s	May be	MB
It is not	TsNd	May be found	MBFnt
It may be	TmB	May have	Mv
It must be	TmsB	May have been	MBn
It must not	TmsN	May not	MnT
It might	T²mT	May you	Mu
It was	T²ls	Might be	MTB
It was said	TlsD	Might have	MTt
It will	Tl	Might not	MTnT
It will not	TlnT	Moral certainty	Mr¹⁄₂sR
It would	Tw(r)	More than one	Mrn(b)N
It would be	TB	Much more	Ch³M
It would have	TwH	Much less than	Ch³⁄₂sN

Must be	MsB	Point of view	Pn V
Must have	MsH	Political party	PlKP
Must not	MsN	Put him	P³m
My dear	MD	Quite well known	KwLNN
My fellow-citizens	MFlSs	Referred to	RF"to"
My own	MN	Right or wrong	RtRNg
Natural consequence	NChrsKns	Right hand	R¹Hnt
Natural history	NChrsR	Seem to be	sMB
Natural selection	NChrshn	Seems to be	sMsB
New Testament	N³sM	Seems to have	sMsH
No better	"no"Btr	Seems to have been	sMsHn(f)
No less than	"no"lsN		
No more	"no"Mr	Set forth	StFTh
Nor is it	Nrst	Shall be	Sh³B
Notary Public	nTPB	Shall be done	Sh³BtN
Of all	"of"l(r)	Shall have	Sh³f
Of his-us	"of"s	Shall not	Sh³nt
Of you	"of"u(d)	She had	Sh¹t
Old Testament	olsM	She may	Sh¹m
On account of	"on"Knt	She may be	Sh¹mB
On all hands	"on"l(l)Ns	She may have	Sh¹mH
On the contrary	"on"KntRR	She may not	Sh¹mN
On the one hand	"on"wNNt	She must	Sh¹mst
On the other hand	"on"Nd	She said	Sh¹st
Once more	wNsM	She says	Sh¹ss
Once or twice	wNsTs	She will	Sh¹l
One or two	wNRT	She would	Sh¹w(r)
Ought not	T¹nT	She would not	Sh¹wo
Ought to	T¹I	Should be	"should"(d)B
Ought to be	T¹B	Should be done	"should"BtN
Ought to have	Tf¹	Should be able	"should"BB
Ought to have been	Tf¹N	Should have	"should"(u)H
Ought to know	T¹I"no"	Should it	"should"(d)T
Our own	R³N	Should not be	"should"(u)oB
Out of	Tf³	Should you	"should"(d)u
Over and above	VrABf	Should you not	"should"(d)uN
Over and over	VrnV	Since that time	Sns¹DhM

So far as	SFrs	Through and through	ThrnTh
So long	SNg	Together with	Gw(l)
So many	SmN	Told him	TltH
So much	SSh	Told it	Tlt$t$
Spirit of Christ	sPt¹Kst	Too much	T³Ch
Spirit of God	sPt¹G	To wit	"to" Wt
Spirit of Jesus	sPtJss	Two or three	Tr³Thr
Sure of	Sh³rf	Under the circumstances	NsTnss
Taking it for granted	TTGrnt		
Take into consideration	TsDshn	Under which	NtCh
		Up stairs	Pstrs
That are	Dh³R	United States	Ys
That is not	Dh³sNt	United States of America	YsM
That it	Dht³		
That it is	Dhts³	United States Senator	YsNdr
That it was	Dh³Tls		
That subject	Dh³sB	Very often	VFn
That you	Dh³u	Was not	Z³nt
Their own	Dhrn	We are	wR³
There are	R³R	We are aware	wRW
There was	R³Z	We are not	wRnT
There will be	R³lB	We can	w(l)K³
There would be	R³B	We could	w(l) "could"
They all	Dhl	We have	wH³
They had	DhHd	We may	wM
They had been	DhHn(b)	We must	wMst
They have	Dhv	We were-would	ww(r)
They have been	DhvN	We will	wL
They were	Dhw	We will not	wLo
They will	Dhl	Were not	"were"o
They would	Dhw(r)	When it is	wN¹ts
They would not	Dhw(r)o	Whereas	"where"s
This city	DhsStE	Whether or not	Hwnt
This is	Dhss	Which would be	ChB
This morning	DhsMn	Which will	Chl
This state	DhsSt	While it is	wLds
This subject	DhsSB	Will be	"will" B

Will not	"will"N	You may be	Y³mB
Would not	"would"N	You might be	Y³mTB
You have	Y³f	You must	Ymst
You may	Y³m	Your own	Y³N

BUSINESS PHRASES AND FORMS.

As good as new	s³GsN	Furnish you	FrnY
At an early date	T³n*R*Dt	Greatly oblige	Gr*l*BJ
At hand	T³nt	Hoping to hear from you again	HPHruGn
At liberty	T³B		
At owner's risk	T³nsK	Hoping to hear from you soon	HPHrusN
At the present writing	T³PsRNg		
		I am in receipt	IM³RSt
At the rate of	T³Rd	If you please	FlPs
At this station	T³DhsSshn	Inclosed we send you	NKlsNu
At your earliest convenience	T³RsVn	In compliance with your request	NPlNsYR-Klst
Balance due	BlsD	In our line	NrN
Be able	B*B*	In reply	NPl
Be good enough	BGNv	In reply to your	NPlY
Bill of lading	B*l*L	Into the matter	nT¹tM
By express	B¹sPs	Just received	JstRSf
By mail	BMl	Let us know	"let"s"no"
By this mail	BsM*l*	List price	LstPs
Call your attention	K*l*uTshn	Locomotive	*l*MTf
C.O.D.	SoD	Meet your approval	MTuPf
Deferred payments	D*F*rPs	Much obliged	Ch³BJ
Do so	Ds	Much pleased	Ch³Pst
Duly received	DRSf	Musical instruments	M³sNsts
Early as possible	*R*lsPsB	Musical merchandise	M³sM
Early attention	*R* *l*shn	No doubt	"no"Dt
Expressage	S*P*sZh	One per cent. per month	wNPsPM
Express agent	S*P*sZhnt		
Express charges	S*P*sShs	Owners' risk	Nrs*R*sK
First class	*F*stKs	Per cent.	Ps
For sale	FS	Please accept	PlsKsPt

Please let us know	Pls*l*(d)s"no"	We are much pleased	"we" R^3Ch-Pst
Please return to us	PlsRRnts		
Please send us	PlsNs	We are willing to	"we" R^3l- "to"
Please sign	PlsN		
Privilege of examination	Pr*t*JsMn	We feel	*w*(l)F¹*l*
		We inclose	wN¹Kls
Replying to your	RP*l*Y	We may be able	wMB*B*
Retail price	Rt*L*Ps	We regret to say	*w*(l)RGr-S
Send you	Sntu	We shall be pleased	*w*Sh³BPst
Serious inconvenience	SrsN *V*n	We shall have	*w*Shf³
		We will	wL¹
Shipping receipt	Shst¹	We will say	wL¹S
Some time since	sMMsNs	We will sell you	wL¹Slu
Style one	stLwN	We would like	"we"*w*(r)K
Take the liberty	TB	Wholesale	H*l*s*l*
Taken the liberty	TnB	You are at liberty	Y³TB
Too late	T³*L*d	You may be able	Y³mB*B*
Very much pleased	VSh*P*st	Your esteemed favor	Y³sMdFf
Very well	V*l*	Your favor	Yf³
Was received	Z³Sf	Your kind favor	Y³Kn*F*
We are glad	"we"R^3GD	Your letter	Y³*l*
We are much obliged	"we"R^3Ch-BJ	Your order	Y³RR
		You will find	u²*l*(d)Fnt

LAW PHRASES AND FORMS.

Aforesaid	FrSt	Best of your knowledge and belief	BsJBf
Anything to do	nTh²D		
As a matter of course	s²MKrs	Beyond a reasonable doubt	BnRsNow
As charged in the complaint	s²ChNPlnt		
		Breach of promise of marriage	BrPMr
Assault and battery	Sl¹*B*		
Attorney-General	TrnJn	By the court	B¹tK
At what time	T³Tm	Can you state	K²sTt
Being called and sworn	BK*l*sRn	Ceased and determined	SsAD
		Change of venue	ChV

Circumstantial evidence	sTn VD	How long have you known	H³Ng"no"n
Client	KlN	I am of the impression	IMMPshn
Considered as read	sDsRd		
Counsel for the defendant	K³sD	I did not	I¹DtN
		I do not	I¹DnT
Counsel for the plaintiff	K³sPf	If anything	FnTh
		In and for	NnF
Cross-examination	KrsMn	In point of fact	NPnF
Defendant's counsel	DsK	In rebuttal	NBtl
Did you ever	Dlf¹	In writing	Nrd:I
District-Attorney	DsTN	Irrelevant and immaterial	RRM
District court	DsK		
Do you know	Dl³I	Is not well taken	s¹Ntw$L$Tn
Do you know anything about	Dl³InThB	Judicial district	JDs
		Justifiable homicide	JsFMsD
Do you live	Dl³ V	Just state	JsTt
Do you think	Dl³Th	Last will and testament	l²(d)slTsM
Duly sworn	DsRn		
Expressed or implied	SPsMPlt	Law	L¹(f)
		Leasehold	L¹sHt
For life	FF	Legal and personal representative	LGlPsR
Gentlemen of the jury	JnJR		
		Letters of administration	LRsDsR
Good and competent evidence	G³nPt VD		
		Manslaughter	M³sLR
Goods and chattels	G³sChls	Matter in controversy	M³.Knt Vr
Go on and state	G³Nst		
Grant, bargain and sell	GrnBSl	Matter of fact	M³F
		Matter of law	M³L
Habeas corpus	HBsK	May it please your honor	MPlsN
Handwriting	H³nRNg		
Heirs, executors, administrators, and assigns	RsKsDsNs	Mechanic's lien	MKslN
		Money had and received	mNHRSf
How long have you been	H³Ngn	Motion for a new trial	MsNTrL

Murder in the first degree	MrFrsG	State how	stH³
No, sir	"no"s	State if	stF¹
Not guilty	NtGT	State when	stwN¹
Of and for	"of"nF	State when and where	stwN¹w
On friendly terms	"on"Frn-TRMs	State where	st"where"
On the same day	"on"sMD	State whether	stHw
Party of the first part	P³FstP	Superior court	sP¹K
		Supreme court	sP¹mK
Party of the second part	P³sKP	Taken under advisement	TnNsM
Personal property	PrsP	That he was	Dh³mZ
Plaintiff's counsel	PfsK	That I was	Dh³Z
Pleads guilty	PlsGT	That is to say	Dh³sS
Police court	PlsK	Then and there	DhnAR
Power of attorney	PrfTN	Took possession	T³Psshn
Prisoner at the bar	PrsBR	To the best of my recollection	BsMRshn
Property-holder	PrPHR	Under the influence of liquor	Nt²NsKr
Pursuant to adjournment	PrSnZhn	Uninterrupted possession	NnTPPsS
Quite intimately acquainted	KNtKnt	Upon their own showing	P¹trNSh-e
Real estate	RlS	Verdict	VrK
Revenue	RVN	Verdict for the defendant	VrKD
Right, title and interest	RtTLNst		
Rulings of the court	R³NgsK	Verdict for the plaintiff	VrKPf
Say anything to you	SnThu	Versus	VsS
See him	Sm	Were you there	"were you" R
Sergeant-at-arms	sR³Rms		
Set forth	StFTh	What is your business	T¹sBsNs
Sets forth	SsFTh		
Seized and possessed of	SstPsSf	Where do you live	"w"³(l)V
Something of that kind	SmThDh-Knt	Where do you reside	"w"²(l)RsD

Wilful negligence	"will" *F*1N	Writ of injunction	RtJshn
Words to that ef- fect	} *R*sDh*F*K	Yes, sir	YsR
Writ of error	Rt*RR*	Your honor	Y'N

, NOTE.—Where Stenotypes are carried to the next line below, and hyphens are used, such hyphens do not indicate nearness, except in the case of the phrases "We are willing to," on page 185, and "Something of that kind," on page 187.

Thee
Ish
Zhee
Ess
Zee

190

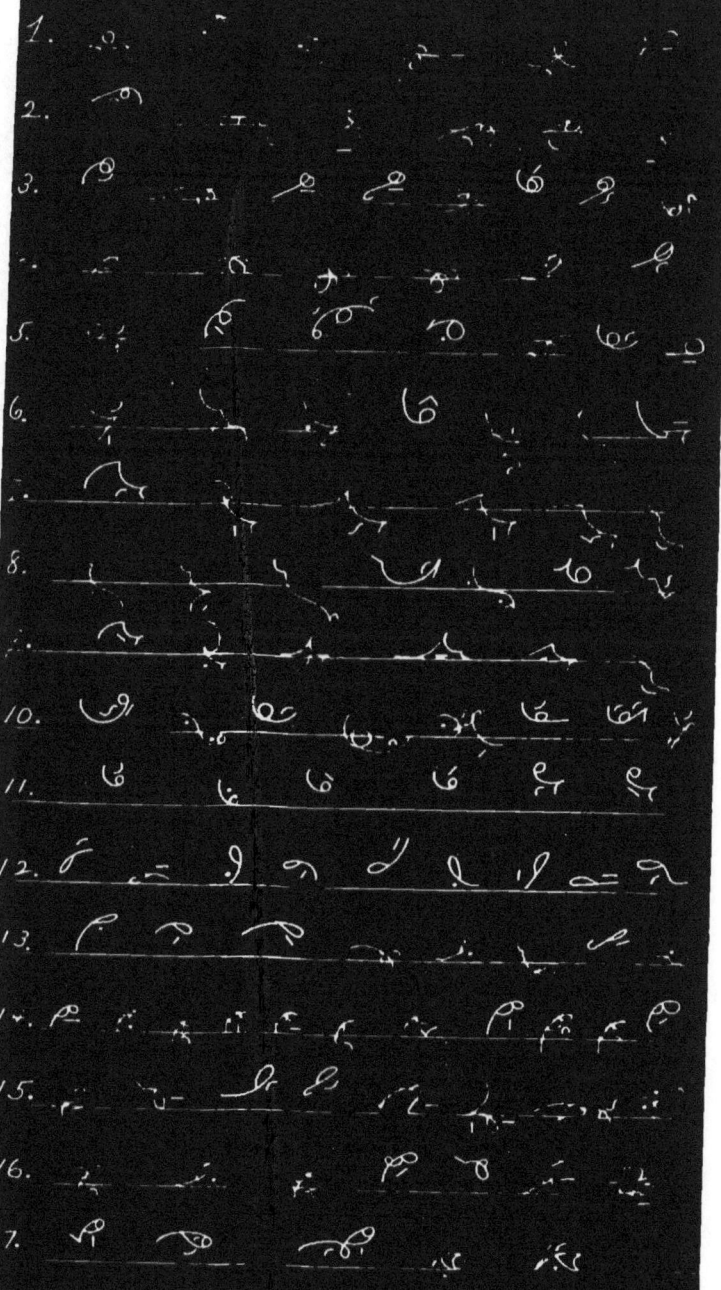

192

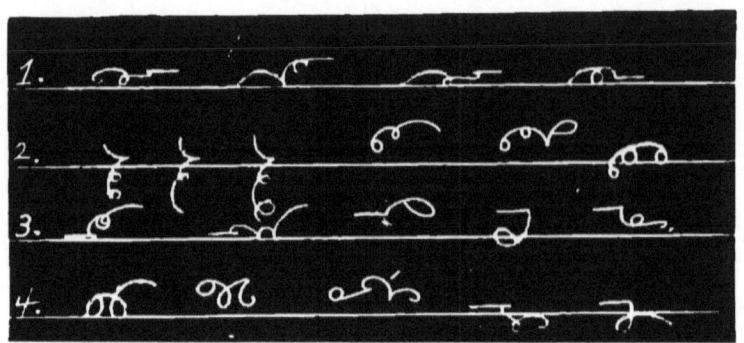

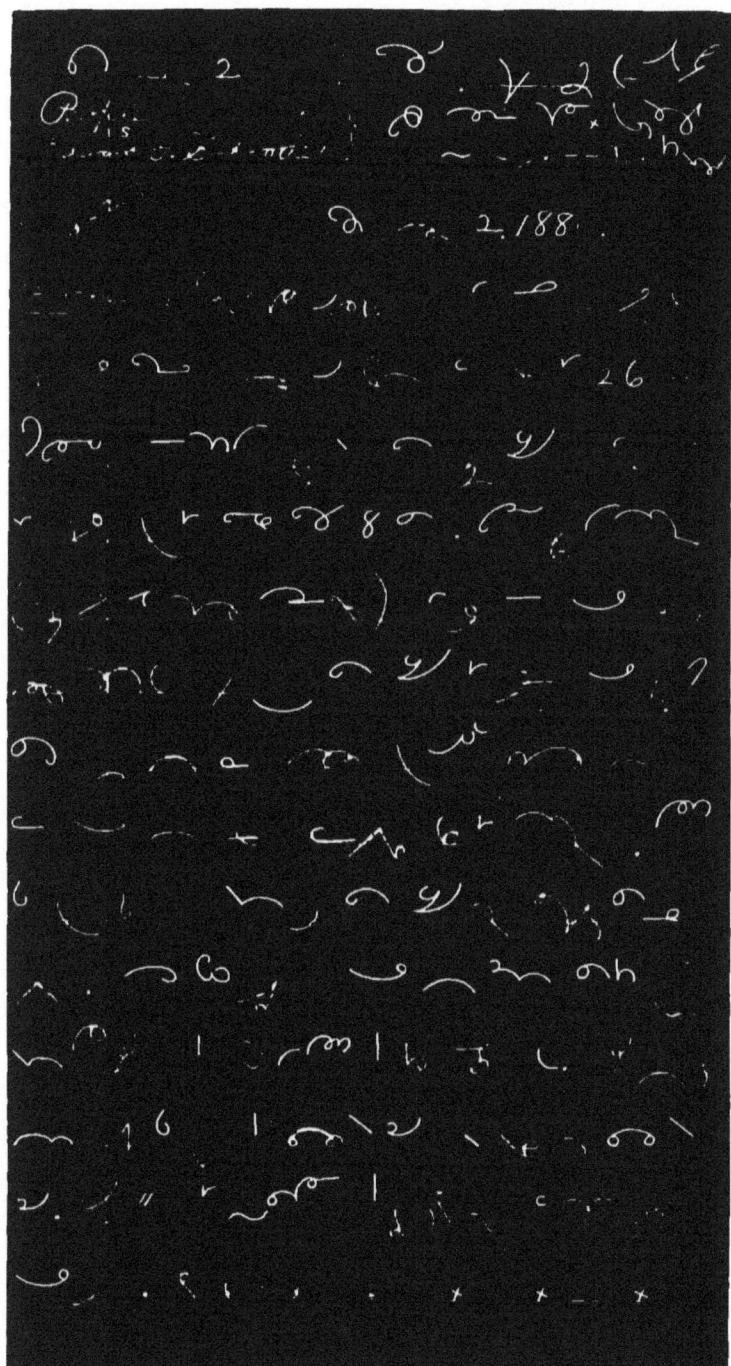

212

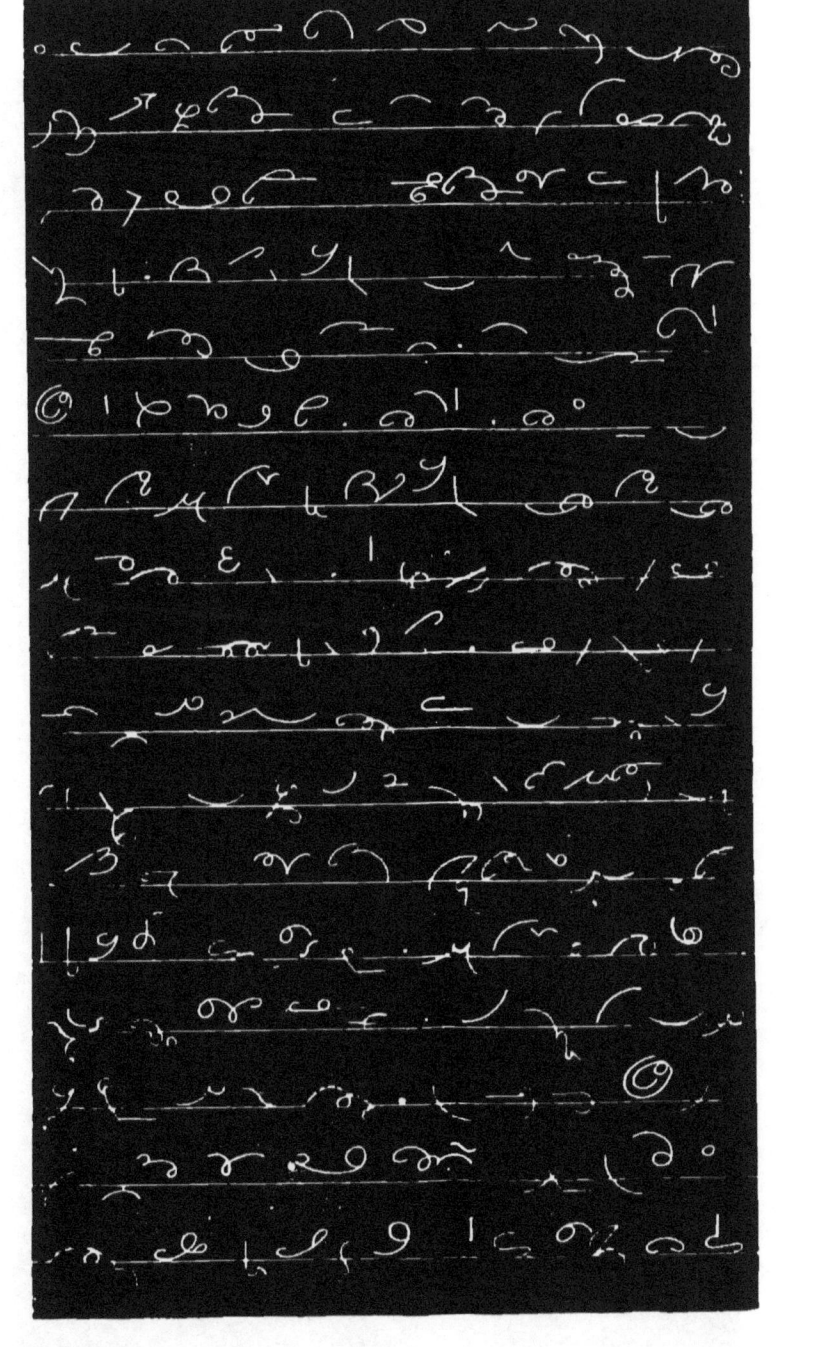

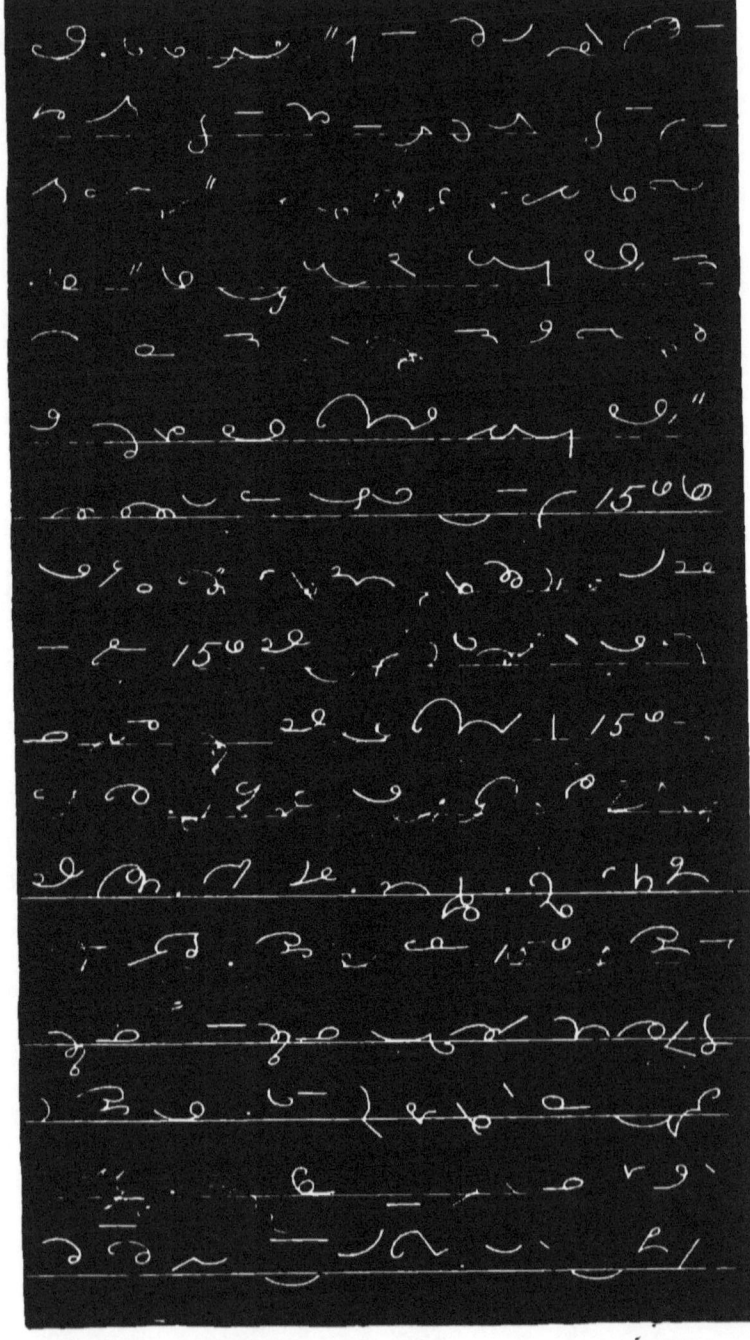

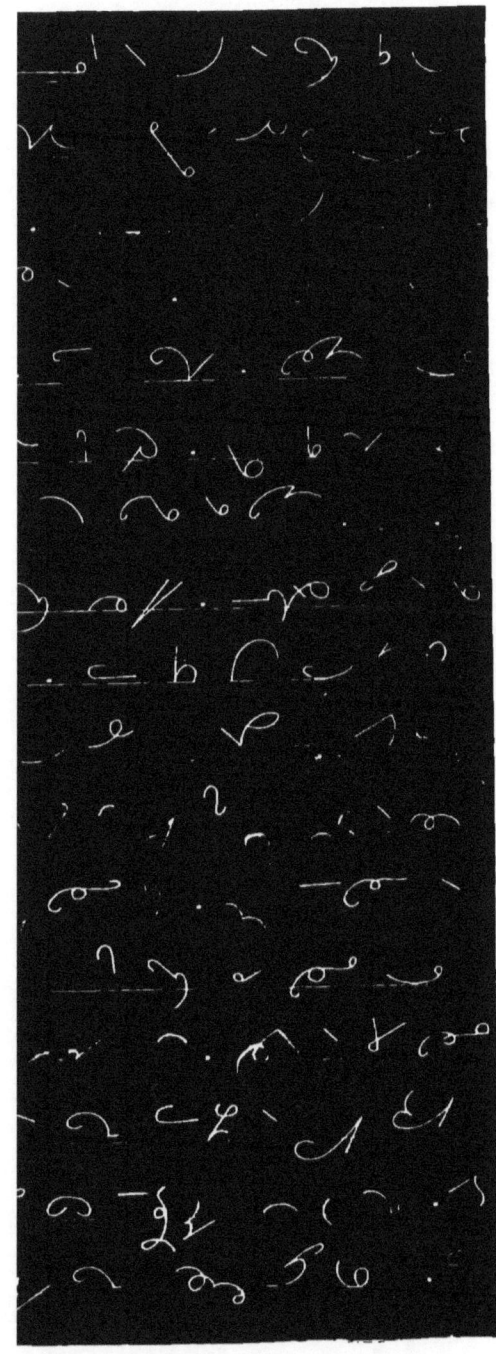

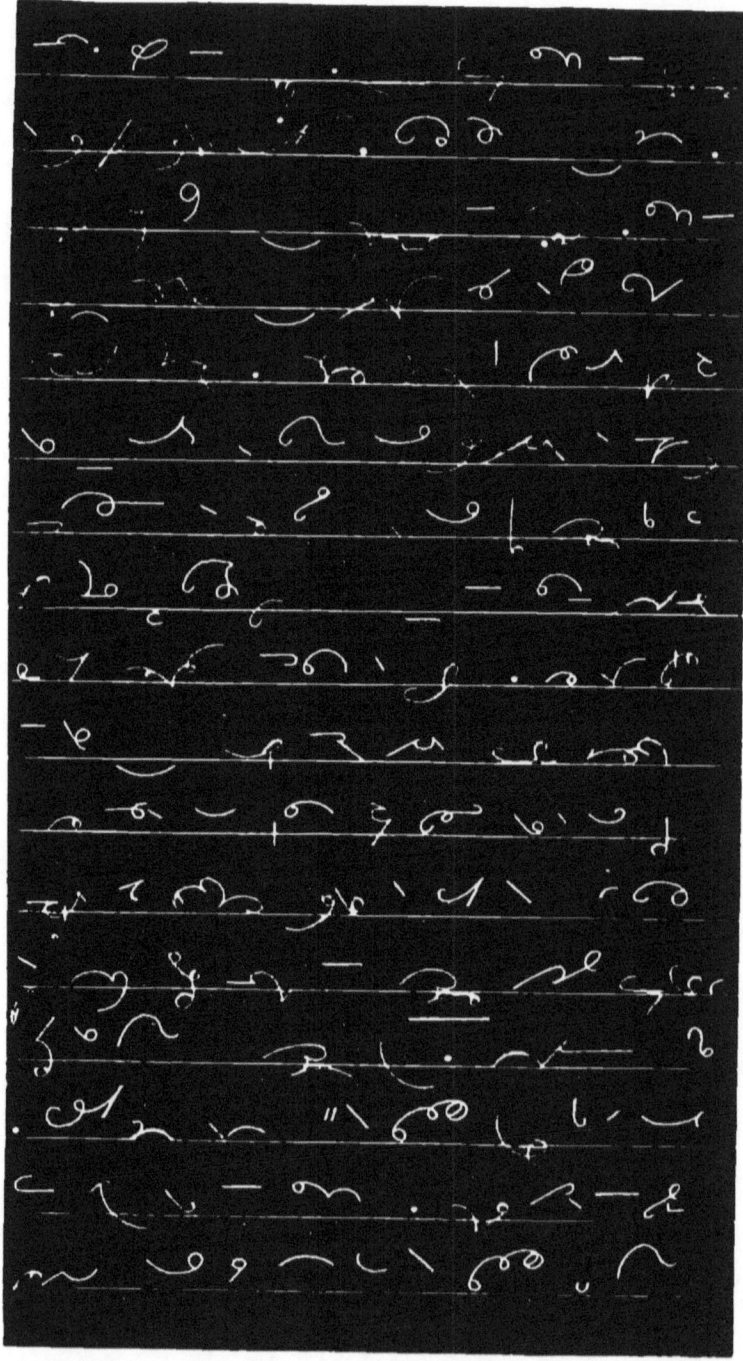

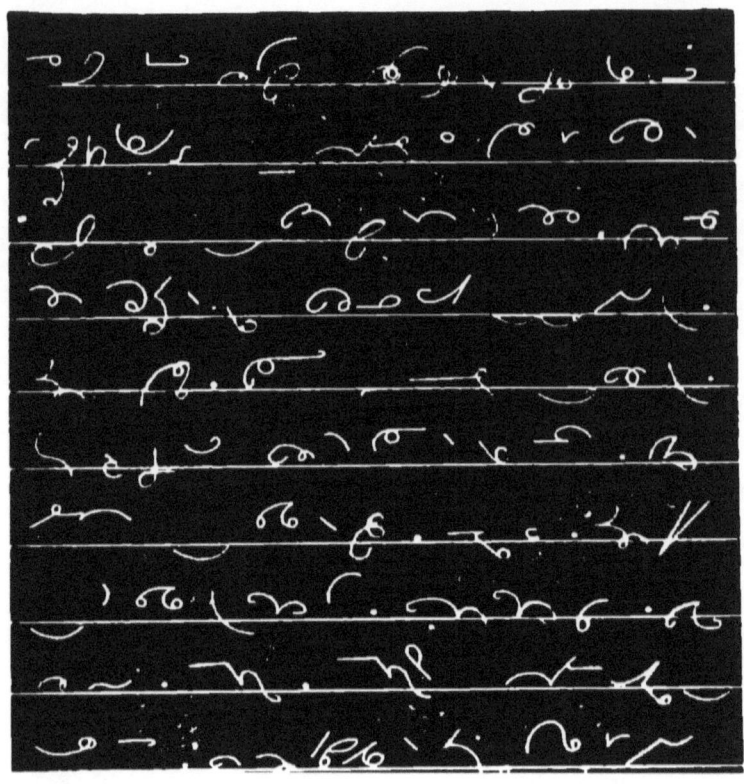

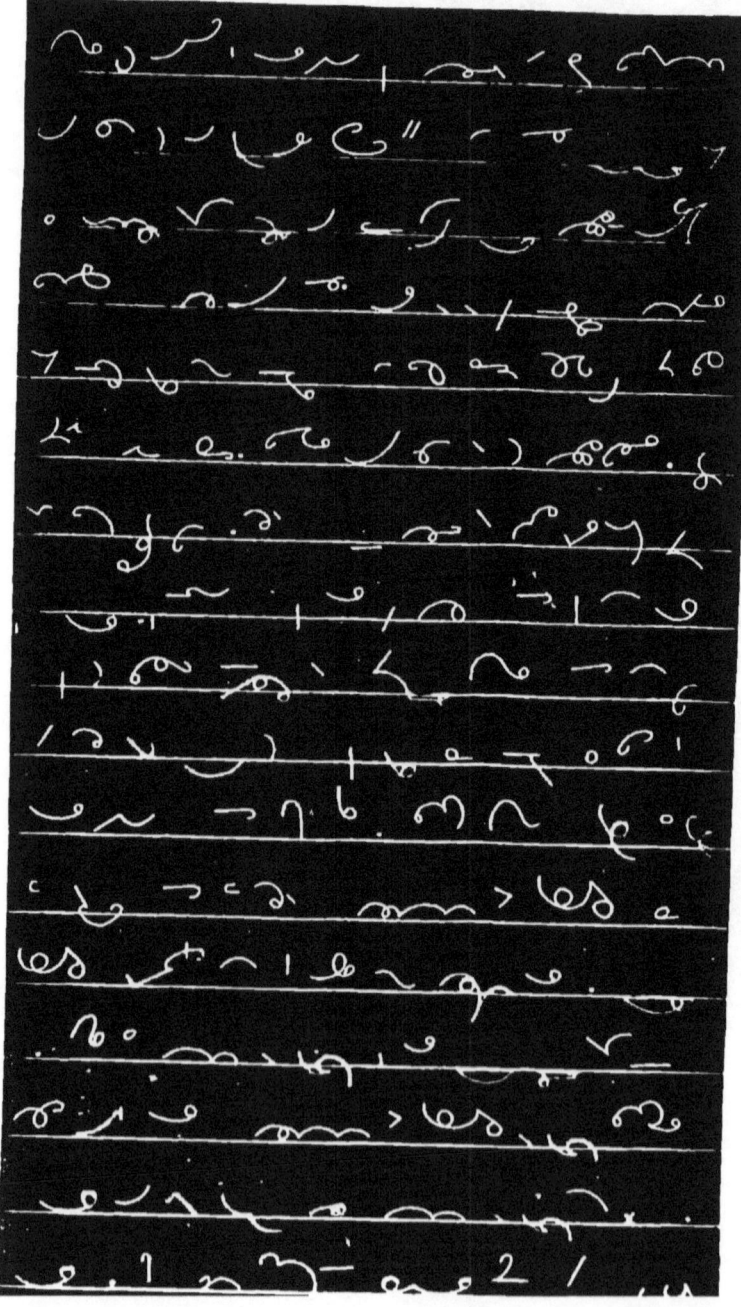

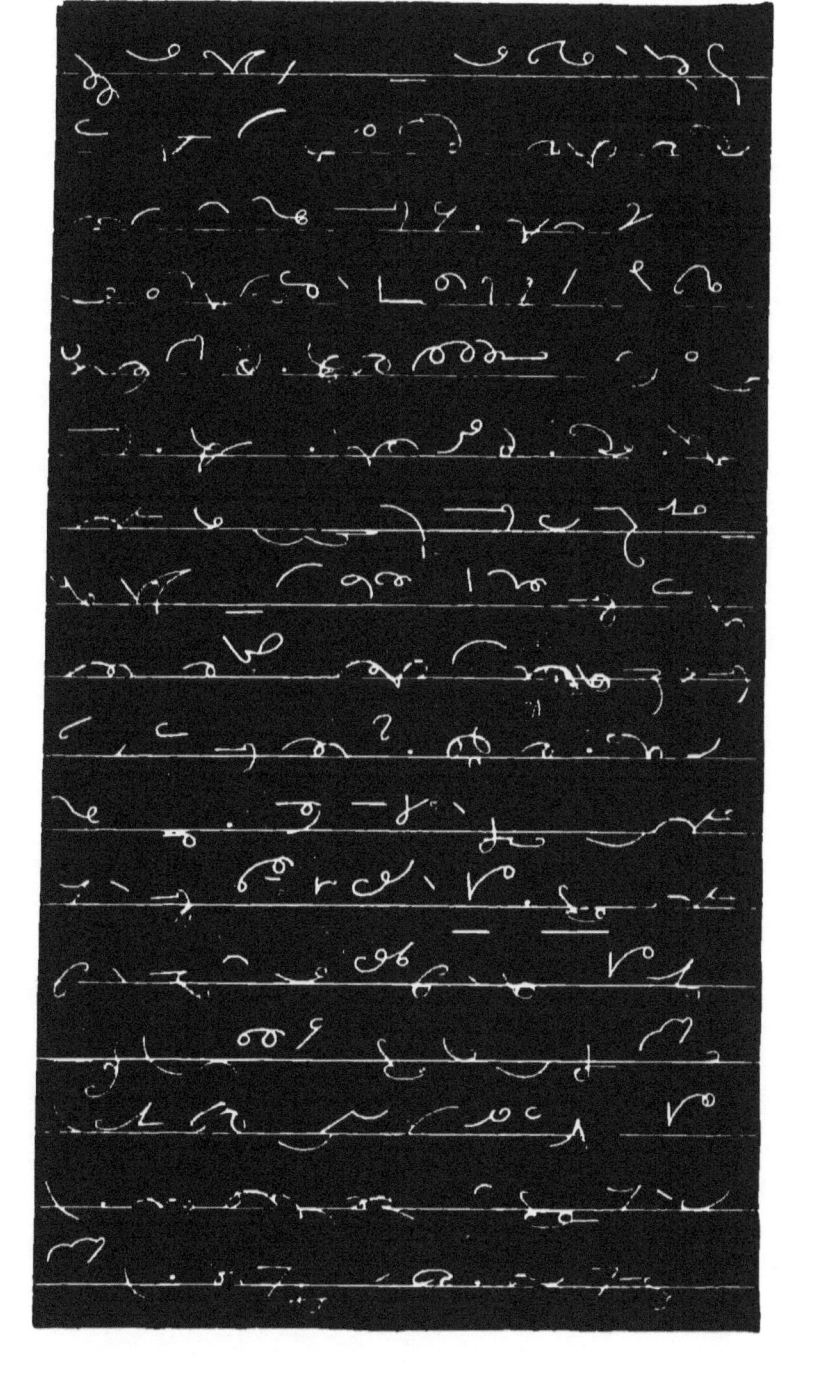

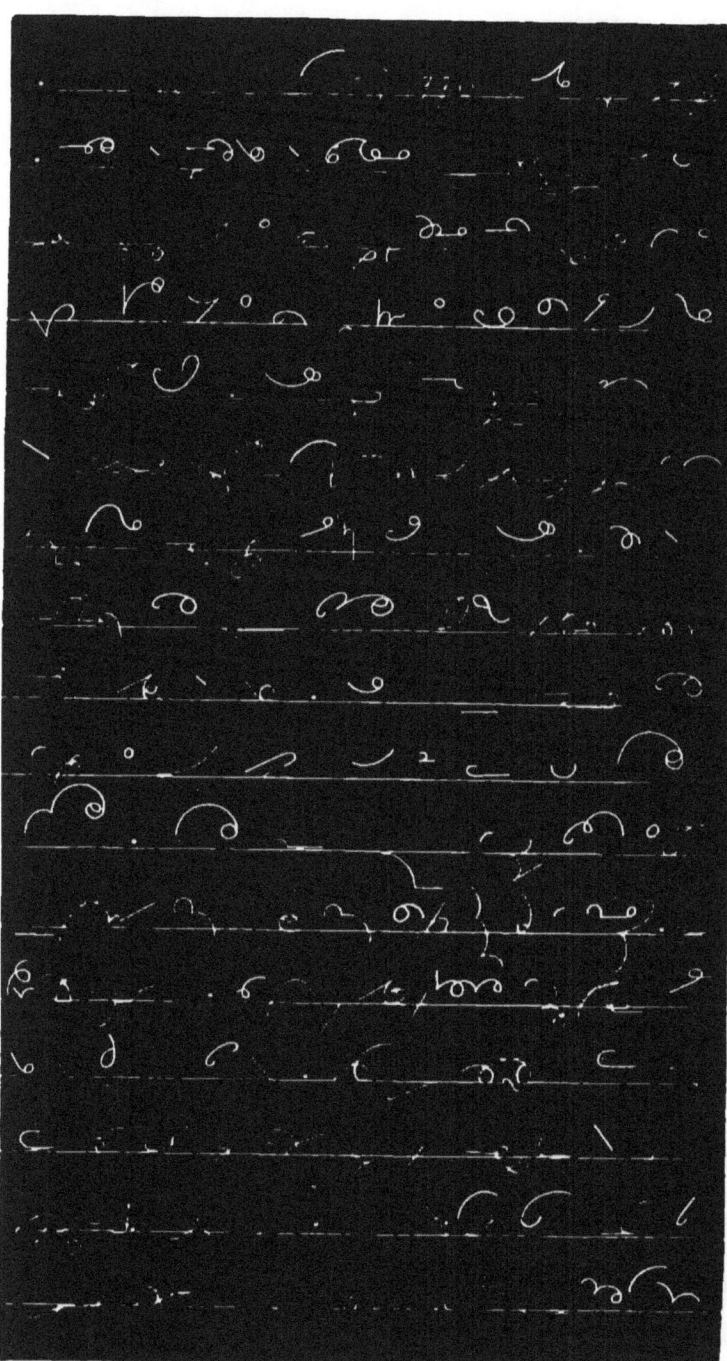

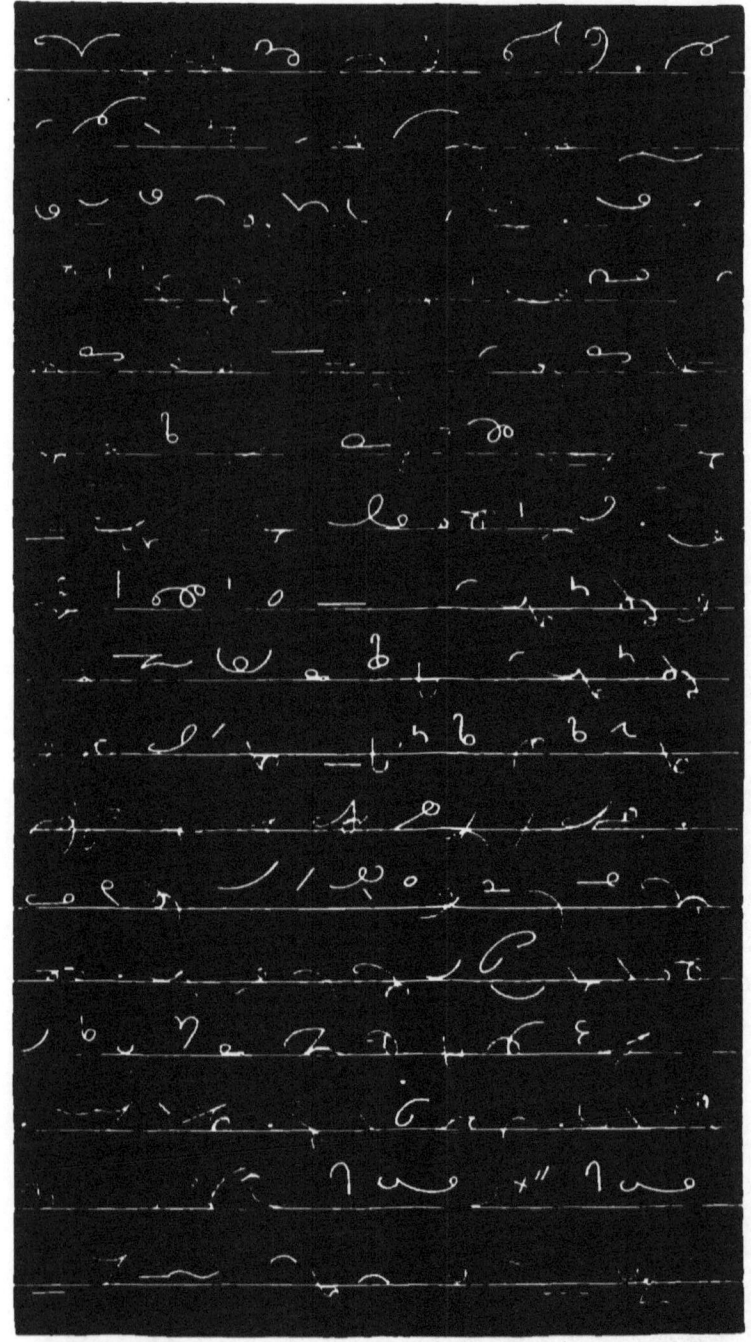

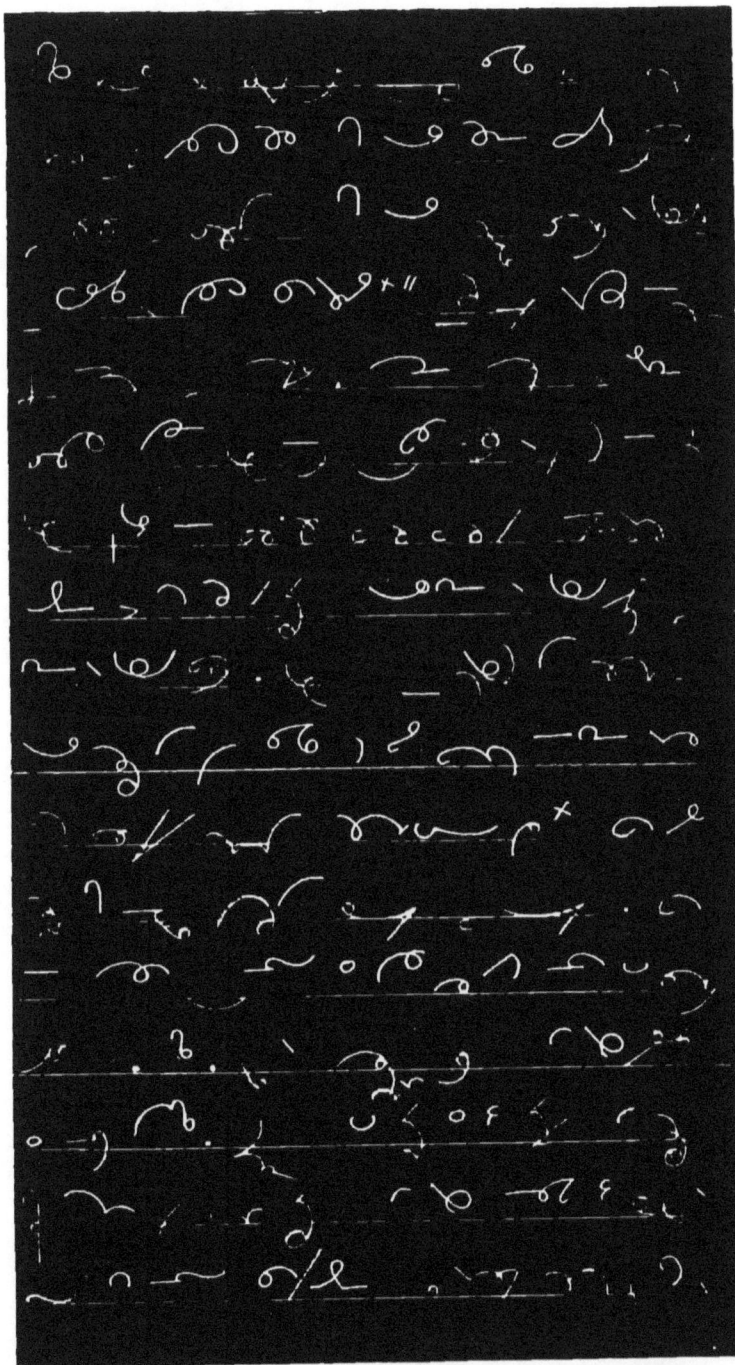

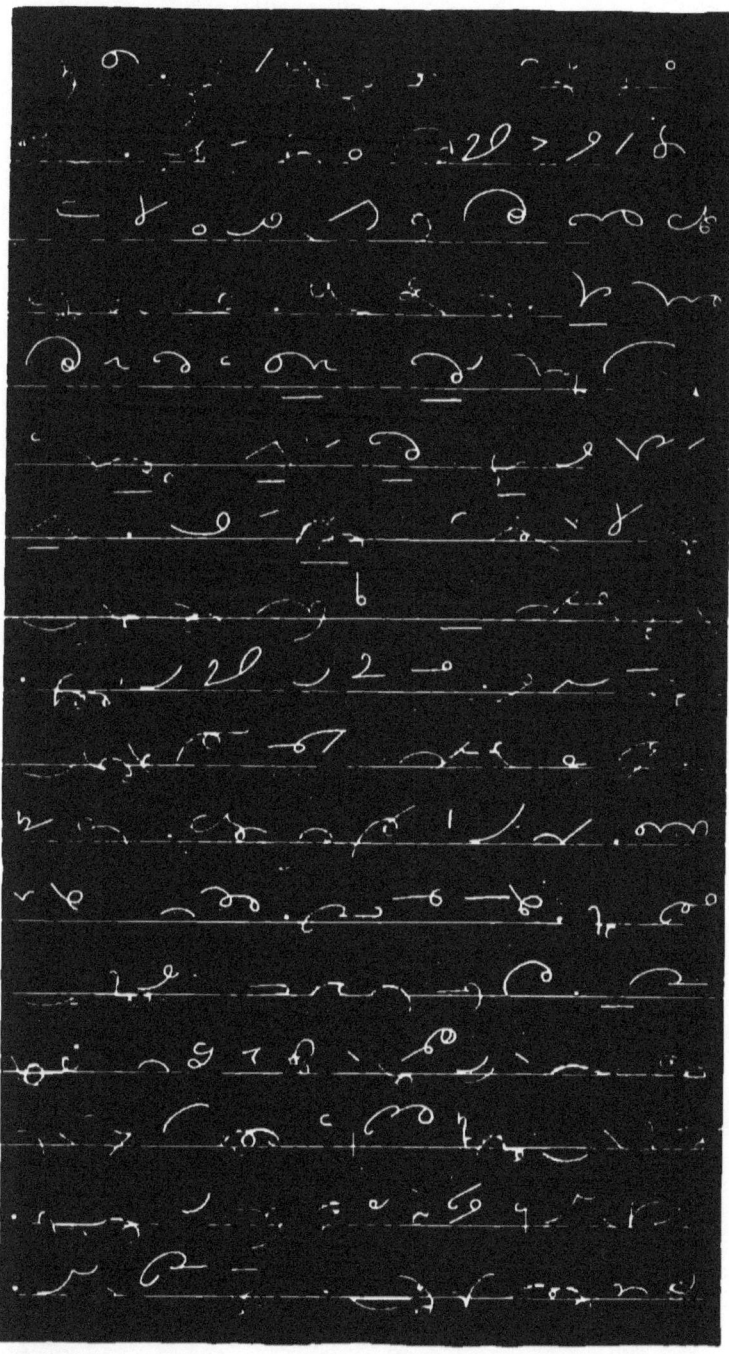

www.ingramcontent.com/pod-product-compliance
Lightning Source LLC
Chambersburg PA
CBHW031735230426
43669CB00007B/355